Old Heath Memories

Patrick Denney

FRT Publications

Acknowledgements

First and foremost I would like to express a special thank you to all those present and past Old Heath residents who feature in this book, for without their help and assistance none of this would have been possible. They have all without exception welcomed me into their homes and have willingly shared with me their treasured family memories and experiences. I am grateful also to those who allowed me to copy and make use of personal family photographs, all of which have proved extremely useful in helping to illustrate this collective story of Old Heath.

The one person featured in the book that I didn't have the good fortune to meet up with was Alfred Mason, who was born as early as 1878. Back in the 1960s, Alfred wrote down some of his memories for publication in the *Colchester Express* newspaper, and he also featured in a book called *The Great English Earthquake* by Peter Haining. I would therefore like to acknowledge the valuable contribution made by these two sources.

Finally, I would like to acknowledge the kind support given by the Old Heath Community Trust who have generously sponsored this project, and also to Fr Richard Tillbrook whose help and unwavering support has been vital in bringing the book to publication.

First published 2016

FRT Publications

13 Abbot's Road, Colchester, Essex, CO2 8BE

British Library Cataloguing in Publication Data.
A catalogue record for this book is available from the British Library.
ISBN 978-0-9552944-1-9

Contents

Introduction

The following collection of memories first began to take shape more than twenty-five years ago when I first became involved in recording oral history. This was in connection with a project to conduct a series of life story interviews depicting life in Colchester in the early years of the twentieth century. And, as one might expect, a fair number of those people interviewed at that time were people from Old Heath, and their memories, largely dealing with life in the area up to the early 1920s, have finally been given their 'voice' in this present publication.

Fast forward to the summer of 2015 and it was decided to add to this earlier group of recordings by conducting a further series of interviews with present day Old Heath residents, and others who have local connections. This second series of interviews, which has taken place in recent months, effectively represents the next generation from the earlier group, thus taking the story up to around the 1960s. In total the memories of over forty Old Heath residents have been recorded and included in the following pages, and with the exception of Alfred Mason, (see Acknowledgements), the oldest person interviewed was born in 1902 and the youngest in 1949. So their collective memories span a time period stretching from the early years of the twentieth century right up to the present day, although the present publication closes the story sometime around the late 1960s. Sadly, of course, many of those whose memories were recorded during the earlier period have since passed away, but from among the present day group, the oldest contributor was eighty-eight years of age at the time of interview, and the youngest sixty-six. Various aspects of local life are depicted including early childhood memories, family life, schooldays, work, wartime and leisure. Many can recall what can only be described today as a bygone age. There were very few cars on the roads and many can recall horse-drawn vehicles delivering provisions directly to your door. Others can remember being able to play ball games in the street outside their homes without any fear of being run down, or injured by traffic. Heating in the home often consisted of nothing more than a single coal fire in the living room, and the family wash was all done by hand using coppers, tubs and mangles. Some can even recall having no water laid onto their home whatsoever, and instead would have to collect it in buckets from a standpipe outside. And unless you were fortunate enough to have a bathroom fitted in your home, bath night often involved making do with a tin bath in front of the fire. Also for many families an outside toilet was considered the norm and it often consisted of a small ramshackle building hidden away somewhere up the garden. Regarding leisure time spent in the home, there were no televisions or other modern forms of amusement, and entertainment in the home was very much what you made it. In fact, many can recall the highlight of the evening being seated round the family table playing games or cards.

This book will certainly appeal to those who know Old Heath, but also to others who enjoy taking a nostalgic stroll down memory lane.

Patrick Denney (June 2016)

Chapter One

Home & Family

A Donkey and Cart

I was born at the Hythe in 1878 and when I was two years old my parents moved to the village of Old Heath, where my father and his brother ran a market garden. His only means of transport at the time was a donkey and cart, and there were many of these to be seen in and around the village at that time. This donkey and cart is among my earliest memories and I can recall when I was about five years of age being allowed go with mother and aunt Emily in the donkey cart to North Station to see my aunt off on the train to Suffolk.

Alfred Mason (born 1878)

Our Toilet was at the Top of the Garden

I was born at Cockwatch Farm on the Mersea Road where my father kept about 700 pigs. When the First World War came along the government took the farm over and we had to move out to Old Heath. First of all we went into a little cottage next to the Bell, and then into 6 Moy's Cottages [now 278 Old Heath Road]. Mr Richardson, from Grange Farm, had bought all six of Moy's Cottages for £600. There was no bathroom in the house and our toilet was outside at the top of the garden. When we wanted to use it we had to take a pail of water with us to flush it. Many of the houses in Old Heath, especially those up on the Heath [near the Bell], used to have their toilets emptied by Mr Robinson from Battleswick Farm. He used to take it away free of charge and spread it on his fields.

Fred Johnson (born 1902)

Old Heath was Almost Like a Separate Village

The bungalow where I live now [350 Old Heath Road] was newly built when we moved in. We heard that they where going to build on 'Johnson's Ground' - a field belonging to Mr and Mrs Johnson, and we paid £2,000 for it. When we first moved into Old Heath [Canwick Grove] in the 1930s there were hardly any houses there, and there were no houses down at Barn Hall Estate. I can remember those being built - it was just trees there before that and it used to be lovely. Old Heath was almost like a separate village.

Doris Thimblethorpe (born 1903)

We Had to Flush the Toilet with a Bucket

Our house at Moy's Cottages didn't have too many conveniences. Although our toilet was connected to the sewer, we had to flush the water down with a bucket. On wash day the water was heated in a copper and then the linen was scrubbed in a galvanised bath using either yellow or primrose soap - we had no soap powders in those days. Even for bathing we had to use the galvanised bath. You could stand up in it but you couldn't sit down. The young ones could sit in the bath but the adults had to be on their knees. However, they kept themselves clean.

Les Crick (born 1906)

Moy's Cottages - now 274-284 Old Heath Road - but formerly 2-12 Old Heath.

We Used Candles to Go to Bed

I was born at 42 Fingringhoe Road in 1915. Our house had no bathroom and we had to use a tin bath in front of the fire on Friday nights. The water was heated in a copper which had a fire underneath. The youngest would be bathed first and then got to bed, and then the boys as they came home would have theirs. I suppose mum and dad had theirs in the same way. We only had a bath once a week. We had gas lighting downstairs - just one in both the front and back rooms, otherwise we used candles. I used to have a candle to go to bed. My mother would do the wash on a Monday. The copper would be lit and she would boil up the water. We had an oval-shaped bath which was put on a stool for her to put the washing in. It took her nearly all day to get through it all, and then all the scrubbing had to be done. When the washing had all been rinsed, it was all put through a big wooden mangle to get the water out before it was hung out on the line.

Phyllis Gibbins (born 1915)

Our Shop was the First to Have a Petrol Pump

I was born at Dedham and was about twelve months old when we moved to Old Heath. My father's name was McGregor Mason and he owned a number of businesses in the town repairing cars and motorcycles. The one in Old Heath was the first shop to have a petrol pump. The shop was connected to the house where we lived. The original shop was just like one big shed and during the First World War we used to have a little tent alongside it where we would hire out cycles to the army, who were stationed up on Middlewick.

Steve Mason (born 1906)

McGregor Mason's original garage in Old Heath dating from around 1920. Mr Mason is seen standing just to the right of the car, with his son Steve standing to his left.

We Had No Water Indoors

We lived at 39 Wick Lane [now 4 Wick Road] which was a two up, two down in a row of four. We had no water indoors and there was just a single tap outside which served all four houses and we had to carry the water inside in buckets. I can remember the tap being wrapped up in the winter to stop it freezing. The toilet was out the back and you needed a torch if you went out at night. It had two wooden seats and they were scrubbed every week to keep them clean. We had no soft toilet paper in those days and most people would use newspaper - cut up into squares and threaded on a string and hung up. Sometimes we would use tissue paper that the bread was wrapped in. My mother kept all that for the toilet, but it didn't last long.

Edna Mills (born 1918)

We Didn't Eat Tin Stuff Like They Do Today

I was born in Old Heath in one of the little cottages opposite the Bell. I had five sisters and four brothers. We had no running water - just a tap and a toilet outside. When I look back I think that we were much healthier then because you wouldn't sit down and eat all the tin stuff like we do today.

Elsie Seaborne (born 1908)

Edna Mills, pictured in 1993 aged seventy-five.

We Always Had Big Hams Hanging Up Around the Fireplace

My uncle used to come and kill the pigs that we kept at Old Heath. Mother would heat up the boiler in the kitchen and when uncle came to kill the pig he would hit it over the head with a mallet, lay it out on a bench, and then cut its throat and let all the blood pour out - hence thesaying'to bleed like a pig'. Then he would put it in a tub of boiling water and scrape it to get all the hair off and then he would hang it up on two hooks and leave it hanging overnight. The next day, when it was cold, he would cut it up. He would cut it right down the centre into halves and then he would joint it. They would then be put into big pans to salt them. We always had big hams hanging up around the fireplace. They were all smoke-dried and you could cut off big thick slices of bacon whenever you wanted it. And it was real bacon in those days - you don't see it today.

Fred Johnson (born 1902)

We had Salt and Pepper Mash for Breakfast

We didn't live very richly in those days because there wasn't the money coming in. At one time my mother took in washing for the ladies in the big houses in Colchester, which comprised their general washing and servants' aprons. So she was able to get a little money from that. We were well looked after but we didn't have big expensive meals and would have lots of bread and jam and sometimes porridge. For breakfast we would often have salt and pepper mash. The bread would be soaked in hot water and have a little bit of butter and a bit of seasoning added. It was hot and served the purpose of warming you up to start the day - and if you could afford it, you would have milk sop

Les Crick (born 1906)

The Sheets Didn't Have to be Ironed

When the washing had been rinsed it was put through the mangle. And when the sheets were dry they also went through the mangle to straighten them out so they didn't have to be ironed. The clothes were then put on the line which was from one end of the garden to the other. We also had a clothes horse for airing the clothes indoors, and I can always remember there being two lines up across the living room. The fire was going and there was always stuff airing there.

Edna Mills (born 1918)

Les Crick, c.1990.

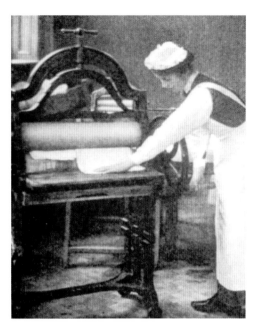

Putting the washing through the mangle.

We Had to Pump the Hot Water Upstairs

We moved to Old Heath when I was about eight years old and went to live at 160 Speedwell Road. When you went in the front door you went straight upstairs. The living room door was on the right, and then out of that was another door leading into the kitchen. And then we had to go out through the back door to get to the toilet. The bathroom was upstairs and there were just two bedrooms. There was a cold tap on the bath but we had to pump the hot water from downstairs. This was from the copper which was in the kitchen and it had a fire underneath which had to be lit. The copper was also used to boil the washing up on wash day, and for boiling the water used for washing and bathing. We had to fill the copper with cold water collected from the tap and carry it to the copper in buckets, and when the water was heated we had to pump it up to the bath.

Gladys Rudd (born 1927)

The House Was Absolutely Freezing

All we had in the house was a coal fire in the dining room and the rest of the house was absolutely freezing - it was like an ice box. Every morning in the winter the windows in the bedrooms were completely iced up. You would have to scratch it off. We used to get undressed for bed downstairs in front of the fire and then run upstairs and get into bed. We had gloves, socks and hot water bottles to help keep us warm. Our front living room was only used at Christmas and we would have a fire in there then.

Margaret Moss (born 1934)

All the Cooking Was Done on an Open Fire

Breakfast was usually bread and jam, or sometimes toast and cheese. For dinner you would get anything that was cookable, all kinds of vegetables because there were plenty around - fairly cheap. And tea was more or less a repetition of breakfast. All the cooking was done on an open fire. We had no electric lighting and had to use paraffin lamps, or candles.

Steve Mason (born 1906)

D'arcy Road Was Just Like a Field
I moved into 1 D'arcy Road when I was six weeks old. My parents had the house built from new. They paid £70 for the land and then paid local builder, Charlie Fisher, £400 to build it. It was a three-bedroom house which included a bathroom upstairs - although the toilet was outside. The water for the bath was heated by a gas geyser which hung over the bath. We only had coal fires for heating - mainly just in the living room. The coal was delivered by horse and cart and was kept in a little shed out the back. When I was a child, D'arcy Road was just like a field and not very well made up. There were only four houses on the left hand side as you go up, and there there were no more houses built on that side until the people who lived in Abbot's Road sold off some of the land at the back of their houses. There were about eighteen houses on the right side of the road, with us living in the first one. In fact, when I was young there still used to be gates at the bottom of D'arcy Road, which were just about hanging on their hinges, from the days when the land was part of a large field.

Maureen Ruddock (born 1935)

We Used to Cut Our Old Clothes Up to Make Rugs
When I was young all our old clothes used to be cut up and made into rugs. We used to cover the floors with them in those days. Otherwise you would cut out an old corn sack and use that - because they were all stone floors then. I can remember my mother getting down on her hands and knees with a bucket of soapy water and scrubbing the floors with a scrubbing brush. There were no vacuum cleaners or things like that in those days.

Fred Johnson (born 1902)

The Washing Was All Done by Hand
Monday was wash day and it was all done by hand. The copper was lit to heat the water. Mother would then put the soap powder in and then take her copper-stick and stir the washing with it - this would be for the sheets - and then she would use some of the water to put in the sink and wash other things by hand in there. And she had a mangle - a big wooden mangle - that she used to put the clothes in and turn the handle round, and there would be a bucket underneath to catch the water. And I can remember turning the handle of the mangle for my mother and seeing all the clothes go through and the water coming out underneath. I can particularly remember the winter of 1947 which was a very cold winter, and I can remember mum hanging the washing out and when she went to get it in everything was completely frozen and I can remember her just standing this frozen washing in the corner of the room.

Janet Rayner (1937)

Everyone Would Have Their Bath at the Same Time
Bath night was Saturday night - once a week - that was all. Everyone would have their bath at the same time. And although we had to share the water in those days, I think people are very wasteful now. I mean, dad used to use the water that was left over from the bath for watering his garden. When we were very little us children used to have a little tin bath in front of the fire.

Gladys Rudd (born 1927)

We Had a Wooden Top Over the Bath
I lived at 11 Cavendish Avenue as a child in a two-bedroom house. We had a front room which was only ever used at Christmas time. In the back room we had the gas cooker in a cupboard next to the fireplace, and then a little scullery with a bath in which had a wooden top on so you could work there when you were not using it. There was also a copper in the scullery where we would heat the water, and then we had to ladle it into the bath with kettles and saucepans.

Margaret Madden (born 1944)

Maureen Ruddock pictured in October 2015.

Below: D'arcy Road as seen in October 2015. When building work began here in the 1930s, the road was not made up and the site was part of a large field. Maureen Ruddock can remember the old field gates still being in place at the bottom of the road when she first lived here.

Janet Read, pictured in November 2015.   Phyllis Gibbins, c.1990.

We Always Had to Say Grace
We always had to say grace before starting meals and you were not allowed to start until everyone else was ready. If you did you got your fingers rapped with a spoon or something. And you didn't get down from the table until everyone was finished, unless there was a special exception, such as something on at the Chapel.

Phyllis Gibbins (born 1915)

You Could Furnish a House for About £50
I met my wife Lilian Oakley in 1927 and we finally got married in 1934. We managed to buy a plot of land in Old Heath Road and built our own house on it [215 Old Heath Road]. We had to pay £450 to have the house built - which was a lot of money in those days. But it was a time when furniture was very cheap and you could furnish a home for about £50. We paid £10 for a carpet and £15 for a three-piece suite. I did wonder if I would ever be able to pay for the house and we never paid anything off during the war.

Les Crick (born 1906)

I Had a Wonderful Childhood with All the Livestock
I was born in the front room of the house where I live now at 326 Old Heath Road. My parents had a market garden where they grew all their own vegetables and kept livestock. I had a wonderful childhood because we had pigs, cows and, of course, chickens and turkeys. My sister Wendy and I led a very free life really. My dad also had horses and during the war they had a horse and cart which they would take round Old Heath selling their vegetables. It was my mum who used to drive the horse and cart, because my dad had to stay in the garden and work the land. I think that we had about ten acres.

Janet Read (born 1943)

We Took Candles Upstairs to Bed
My earliest memories of lighting in the house were gas lights in the kitchen and in the front room. They used to be fitted on the side of the chimney breast and you would swing them out and light them with a match. We used candles when we went upstairs to bed. The only heating that we had was from a coal fire, but sometimes mum would light the oven and leave the door open to warm the room.

Keith Moss (born 1934)

My House Used to be the Village School

I married my husband Cyril Johnson in 1939 and we moved into Savill Cottage [326 Old Heath Road] in 1943. In earlier times the building had been used as the local school which had preceded the church school over the road. When we first arrived here the furniture was all covered in sheets and the old boy who used to live here only lived in part of the old schoolroom at the back, with his bed located in one corner of the room. And that was where he lived - he never came into the rest of the house after his sister died. Where we are sitting now at the front of the house was part of the headmaster's accommodation, and from here it led into the old schoolroom. There used to be double doors where the pupils used to enter the building and then steps leading up to the classroom. The old school consisted of one large room with a high ceiling and the bricks on the floor were just laid on sand. There were four classrooms within this one large room and they were divided by partitions which you could look over. At the side of the house, where the children used to come in, was a bell on the wall which was rung as a school bell.

Edith Johnson (born 1908)

Right: Edith Johnson.

Below: Savill Cottage which began life as the first purpose-built school in Old Heath. A note from the diary of James Ashwell Tabor records the date that the school opened -
"Took possession of the New School Room, 20 November 1837"
The headmaster's study was on the ground floor to the right of the front door, and the schoolroom was located at the rear of the building.

We Used to Wake Up to Find Cows in the Garden
I was born at 26 Speedwell Road. I had two younger brothers and two younger sisters, so there were seven of us including mum and dad. Us three girls slept in one bedroom, my two brothers were in another with mum and dad in the other. We only had one coal fire to heat the house and it was always cold in the bedrooms, with ice on the inside of the windows some mornings. We had what we used to call the 'coal hole' at the back of the kitchen and the coalman used to come through the kitchen and dump the coal out - and that's where we kept it. Our house used to back onto the fields and we often used to wake up in the morning to find cows in the garden. They belonged to Mr Ardley and they used to get through the hedge at the bottom of the garden, but they soon used to disappear when it was milking time.

Sandra Bennett (born 1949)

It Was a Wonderful House Full of Character
My name is Steven Ezekiel Bailey although I'm not sure where the name Ezekiel came from, except that it's from my mother's side of the family. I was born at Birchington in Kent but moved to Colchester in 1951 where my dad had got a job at Old Heath Laundry. We lived in a building called 'Hull House', which was apparently named after a boat which had floundered on the Colne sometime in the past. It was a wonderful house full of character. It had big fire places and one room had wood-panelling with very ornate coving and picture rails. In the kitchen there was a box on the wall above the door into the hall with a servants' buzz-box on, so that when someone in whatever room pushed a button it lit up in the kitchen and you would go and see the master, or whoever, and see what they wanted - but not that we used it!

Steve Bailey (born 1948)

The Geyser Over the Bath Used to Roar Like Mad
I was born at North Walsham in Norfolk but when I was just a few weeks old my parents moved to 310 Old Heath Road. The house was built around the 1930s and was probably by the standard of the day quite a nice house. It had a substantial porch, a hall, a front room, a back room and a kitchen. The toilet was outside in those days and there was a coal house next to that. Upstairs there were three bedrooms and a small bathroom. The bathroom had one of those awful geyser heaters - an absolutely frightening thing - you had to light it with a match and it used to roar like mad and, I think, was in constant danger of blowing up.

Martin Broom (born 1945)

Hull House, Distillery Lane 'a wonderful house full of character'.

Steve Bailey, June 2016.   Martin Broom, February 2016.

We Had a Bath Once a Week
In the winter when we woke it was very cold with ice on the windows, but we were soon to be warmed up as there was always a nice roaring fire to come down to. To get to the toilet we had to go out of our back door and across a short path which led to the outside loo. In the winter, mum used to put an oil table lamp in there which gave a little light and also stopped it from freezing. And when I was small we had no tap indoors. We just had one cold water tap outside to fill a kettle, or a bucket of water. And once a week we used to have a bath in the kitchen. Mum would fill the copper and light it up to heat the water. And that's how we used to have a bath. Wendy and I would get in first and then mum and dad afterwards.

Janet Read (born 1943)

We Used to Get an Orange, an Apple and Some Nuts for Christmas
At Christmas time all the extended family used to come to us at D'arcy Road. We would hang our stockings up on Christmas Eve and we would get an orange, an apple and one or two nuts - and that was about it. We used to decorate the home with paper-chains which we made ourselves, and mother would be busy making Christmas puddings and cakes before the event. And, of course, this was when the front room would be used to entertain at Christmas time.

Maureen Ruddock (born 1935)

We Had Bats in the House
We also had livestock in the house in the form of bats. I can remember my sister and I running round the house, upstairs and down, with tennis-type bats trying to catch them. And we also had plenty of mice coming through the skirting boards - there was always something happening. We had a huge back garden with the house where we used to keep pigs, chickens, rabbits and vegetables. And sometimes we'd be growing salad crops and taking them to Worrell's in St Botolph's Street who used to buy our vegetable and salad stuff. Dad would either buy an in-pig sow and let it have the young, or have a boar come down and service our sow which would then have its own young. And we would grow them on, sell some and keep some for ourselves. Once the pig had been killed we would take it round to the boiler house where we would shave it, prepare it, and then hang it in the outhouse and butcher it. We used to do that ourselves.

Steve Bailey (born 1948)

People Used to Eat a Lot of Rabbit

People used to eat a lot of rabbit in those days - I think that we had it about once a week. I really loved it. I can remember one Christmas time my maternal grandfather, who lived in Yarmouth, putting a big rabbit on a Grey Green bus and then my brother going up town to meet the bus and collecting the rabbit, which was our Christmas dinner. Otherwise, we would have had beef or something like that. You didn't get chicken or turkey much in those days. A chicken would have been a real treat.

Janet Rayner (nee Tyler) (born 1937)

Gladys and Frank Tyler are seen here relaxing with their four children on Gorleston Beach in 1947. The children pictured from the left are: John, Janet, Angela and Michael.

Old Heath Road looking towards Colchester near where Cottage Drive is now, c.1935

Chapter Two

Schooldays

Our School Was Used as a Church on Sundays

When I was about five years old I started at the village school which numbered about thirty pupils, of whom quite a number were rather poorly clad. The school consisted of one main room, and was used on Sundays as a church. Our school desks were placed on a series of rising steps, and the older one got the further one progressed from the front of the room to the back. We had two teachers, mother and daughter, who taught us throughout the whole of our school life until the age of twelve. In warm weather, a large jug of water would be passed round the class, from which the children would drink one after the other. This was certainly not very hygienic judging by present day standards - however we all survived. The jug and water were provided by a kindly resident from her garden well and we were always glad of this cool clear water.

Alfred Mason (born 1878)

St Barnabas' Church as seen in 1894. The church opened in March 1875 and until the construction of the new Board School (seen in the background), doubled up as a school during the week.

We Showed the Children How to Harness a Horse

I remember on one occasion when I was at Old Heath School the children in the class came over to our orchard, opposite the school, and my brother Cyril and I had to show the class how to harness a horse. We showed them all the different parts of a bridle and how to put the harness on, and the collar and saddle. And when they got back in the classroom they had to write an essay on what they had been told.

Fred Johnson (born 1902)

At Playtime the Boys and Girls Were Not Allowed to Mix

I can remember my first day at school when I was five years old. Our teacher, Miss Adams, took hold of my hand and put me on a form. I enjoyed my time at school although I wasn't particularly good at anything. Our headmaster, Mr Bates, was a real gentleman. He used to line us up in the corridor every morning and evening, the girls one side and the boys the other. One day he took hold of my hand and said, 'That's the sort of hand I like to see.' He could also be quite strict at times. We used to have to sing a hymn at morning assembly and he got cross with us once and said that we weren't opening our mouths properly. He said a master once told him that you have to open your mouth wide enough to get a lighted match in it. At playtime the girls were on one side and the boys on the other - we were not allowed to mix. We used to play one game called Stag. One child would start off by trying to catch someone and then both of them would join hands and try to catch someone else. And this would go on until everyone had been caught in a long line of children.

Flossie Lappage (born 1905)

You Would Certainly Get the Cane if You Misbehaved

The teachers were all strict in those days and the children were kept under control - more so perhaps than they are today. You would certainly get the cane if you misbehaved, and if you didn't do very well you'd probably get the dunce's hat and have to sit in the corner. I remember on one occasion we had been given an examination to complete where we were awarded various marks and I got 25 out of 26 - which I thought was ok. I had apparently made one mistake with my long division working out and for that single mistake the teacher gave me a nice stroke of the cane across my hand. So I wasn't too happy about that.

Les Crick (born 1906)

They Used to Give Us a Free Breakfast

I remember at Old Heath school, plain as anything, they used to give us a free breakfast. We would have a mug of cocoa and some bread and plum jam. The teacher gave us that because we hadn't had any breakfast. It was because we were so poor and it's no good saying any different - yet we were not rough. It's no disgrace being poor. We used to look forward to getting it although I think my mother resented it a bit even though she knew it was doing us good.

Elsie Seaborne (born 1908)

We Had a Nice Little Plot of Garden

I started school when I was about six years old. I enjoyed school and we had nice teachers. I remember that my mum walked me down to the school on my first day, but I don't remember much more about it. Our first teacher was Miss Adams who lived in Wimpole Road. She was a nice old girl and she used to treat us very well. From there you gradually went up to the higher classes. We didn't have to wear a uniform and we used to wear clogs - we couldn't afford boots or shoes. We also had a little plot of garden each at the top of the playground and you could grow whatever you liked. I would grow vegetables to eat and to take home.

Steve Mason (born 1906)

Gardening class at Old Heath School sometime around 1905.

My Mother Couldn't Afford to Buy Me a Uniform

The teachers were very strict. I had the cane several times, probably for talking in class. When we got to Standard 5 or 6 we had to sit the exam for Hamilton Road School, which was a secondary school and if you passed you went there. I sat the exam and passed the first part, but as mother couldn't afford to buy the uniform I couldn't go. I was disappointed as my friend was going there and I really would have liked to have gone too.

Phyllis Gibbins (born 1915)

We Were Allowed to Take a Toy or Game to Play With

I was five years old when I started at Old Heath School. The desks in the infants' class were on steps rising towards the back so when you sat at the top you could see all that was going on. Our teacher was Miss Adams who wore a long black robe and had her hair done up in a bun. She also had a cane but she didn't use it on us. On Friday afternoons we were allowed to take a toy or a game that you could play with.

Edna Mills (born 1918)

Phyllis Gibbons (on the right) and her sister Miriam in c.1920.

There Was a Big Blazing Fire in the Classroom
I can remember starting at Old Heath School and going into this big room with a coal fire blazing with a big guard round it. I think that the teacher was a Mrs Gardener. The headmaster was Mr Hindle and there was a Mrs Wright who used to teach us for handicraft. I can always remember her because we made an egg cosy to put on top of your egg. You had to weave the wool through holes onto a card which gave you a framework, and then you just weaved it in and out. I did all the weaving work and the teacher lined it for me. It was a blue colour and when it was finished I took it home and I've still got it around here somewhere.

Frank Gooding (born 1931)

Sometimes Our Milk Would Be Frozen Solid
We used to have a third of a pint of milk every morning and sometimes it would be frozen solid. And some of the children used to get called out and they got a spoonful of cod liver oil and malt. They used to have this big jar of cod liver oil and malt and she used to give them all some of that. I think that may have been for some of the children who were probably under nourished. She used to call these children out by their names and I used to think, 'Cor, I wish I could have some of that.'

Margaret Moss (born 1934)

We Used Sand Trays to Form Our Letters
When I first attended Old Heath School I was put into Miss Gobbold's class, and I can remember that she had lovely golden hair. We had sand trays which we used to form our letters, and we used to play all kinds of games. There was a big fireplace in the classroom and in the winter there would be a big fire on the go and we would all sit round and have stories read. In the afternoon we had little lino mats that we had to lie down on and have a rest.

Joy Cardy (born 1934)

Frank Gooding aged five in 1936.

We Used to Have a Sleep in the Afternoon
I was five when I started at Old Heath School. I can remember sitting in the classroom and having a bottle of milk at break time. We used to go home for dinner and when we came back in the afternoon, we used to have a sleep. There used to be a pile of lino cuttings in the corner of the classroom and we used to have to take one, lay it by our desks, and curl up and try to get to sleep for a little while. This was when I was in the first year infants' class.

Maureen Ruddock (born 1935)

We Had to Say Our Times Tables
Every morning we had assembly where we would sing hymns and the headmaster would report on anything that we needed to know. Then we would go to our classrooms where we had all of our lessons. We always started off with the Register and then we usually said our Times Tables and then various lessons from then on. These would include Maths, English, Geography and Mental Arithmetic. But it always started with the Register and Times Tables. I can also remember that if anyone had a birthday the teacher would bring out this cake from the cupboard - I don't know whether it was made of cardboard or not, but it looked like a real cake. And after we'd all sang 'Happy Birthday' it went back in the cupboard again.

Janet Rayner (born 1937)

We Are Going to Start a Football Team
I remember starting in Miss Adam's class at Old Heath School, who was a lovely teacher. Then there was Mr Holmes, Miss Keeble and best of all Miss McKeever, who was a fantastic teacher. She was the teacher that we had for our last year. She was the assistant headmistress to Mr Hindle, the headmaster. I can remember her wearing a kilt and she was a teacher who could hold your attention. And after the war she said. 'We are going to start a football team', and they got permission to play football on a piece of land off Abbot's Road. So she found an old football, looked up the rules of the game, and we used to play football up there. They never had the playing field like they have now.

Dick Jackson (born 1937)

Margaret Moss, pictured in 1945 aged 11.

I Was Assigned to Old Heath School

After I had completed my teacher training I was assigned to Old Heath School in Colchester. I was given a class of eight year olds and I remember being a little disappointed because I had wanted to teach infants, and I had been given juniors. But it was wartime and you didn't question much at that time - you just got on with it. I had also wanted to teach needlework but there was a very good teacher there already doing it so I didn't get either of my wishes, but I settled down happily for the next two years with that group of children.

Mary Holford (born 1920)

I Had to Teach Them Everything

I was finally appointed to Old Heath School and I've never regretted it. I would have been twenty-one years old when I started there in 1954. I didn't have an interview as such, but I had to go and attend a meeting with the headmaster, Mr Richards. And I started by taking the six year olds which would have been the second year infants class. I remember that the children were starting a new term, and I was as well, and we gradually got into the swing of things and I got to know their names. I had to teach them everything, although we did have an extra teacher in those days who would go round everybody's class in turn, so on the odd occasion we did get a bit of free time.

Anna Streatfield (born 1933)

The Bell Used to Ring at Nine O'Clock

I started school when I was five years old. I think that Miss Leveridge was my first teacher and I can remember playing in little sand pits, and then in the afternoon having a little lay down to go to sleep. And when I was seven I moved up to the juniors. And I can remember having to recite my Times Tables. We all had to sit there and recite the whole thing - they don't do that today do they? The bell used to ring at nine o'clock and we had to line up in the playground and then march off to our classrooms, where we stayed for the whole day.

Margaret Madden (born 1944)

We Had to March Off to the Shelter

When the siren went we all had to march off to the shelter - I think that there were two or three of them at the top of the school playground. We had to go down steps to get in them and there were rows of seats - one down each side and one down the middle, so you would sit facing each other. At the far end was an escape hatch which was more or less a large round pipe like a manhole cover. I remember that I used to take a little tin of sweets down with me in case I got hungry.

Frank Gooding (born 1931)

Margaret Madden aged five.

Above: Miss Mary Holford's first class in 1941.

Right: Mary Holford, pictured in December 2015.

Below: Mary Holford reunited with some of her class of 1941 at a school reunion in 2009.

There Were Forty-seven Children in the Class
My first teaching position was at Old Heath School. I knew nothing about Old Heath at the time. I didn't even know where it was. When I turned up for the interview I knocked on the headmaster's door and he suddenly said, 'Oh dear, I'd forgot that you were coming, do you know anybody on the staff?' I said, 'Yes, I know Anna Hedges.' So he said, 'That's good because I'm busy this afternoon and she can show you round the school.' I still hadn't been formerly interviewed for the job, but I think that he had already decided that I would do. The first class that I taught were second year infants and there were forty-seven children in the class. We were squashed into one of the little partition rooms and it was so crowded that the children in the back row had to climb over all the desks to get out for playtime.

Mary Bareham (born 1934)

Mary Bareham, November 2015.

I Always Looked Forward to Nature Trips
I can remember my first day at school. My mother took me and I screamed my head off and they had a job keeping me there. But my mother just turned round and went home and that was the one and only time that she took me to school. I remember that that I really enjoyed anything to do with nature at school and I always looked forward to nature trips where we would go out as a class and go walkabout. Very often we went towards the Hythe which often meant going past my house, at the Laundry, and I can't remember a time when we didn't detour into our garden. The kids loved the animals and everything that we did there.

Steve Bailey (born 1948)

The School Was Divided into Four Houses
The school was divided into four houses - St George, St Andrew, St Patrick and St David, and I was in St Andrew's House. Our House mistress was Miss McKeever and throughout the year you were given House points for various achievements or activities, and the idea was to see which House could earn the most points by the end of the year. Points could also be taken away for misbehaviour. And the House that received the most points would receive a cup presented to the House Captain at morning assembly.

Martin Broom (born 1945)

I Was in Wellington House
During the war years the House names at Old Heath School were named after aircraft. These were Hurricane (green), Spitfire (red), Wellington (yellow), and Lancaster (blue). I was in Wellington and our colour was yellow. We used to compete against each other on Sports Day, which was held on the Wick and at rounders matches in the school playground.

Dick Jackson (born 1937)

We Used to Sell Apples to the Children Going to School

There used to be more bicycles than cars on the roads in those days. Children just used to come and go as they liked, and it wasn't until my last year at the school that they got their first Lollipop man whose name was Mr Lusted who lived at the bottom of Old Heath Hill, near Cannock Mill. When I was at school sweets were still on ration and in the morning my dad used to have boxes of apples outside the house and the children used to come with their pennies and could have one large apple for a penny, or two small ones for a penny. And they used to take them to school for their break. We used to sell a lot of apples like that.

Janet Read (born 1943)

We Used to Pass Prisoners of War on the Way to School

When I went to school we used to walk through a gate and across some allotments where Cheveling Road is now. They were starting to build the houses there at the time and we used to see German prisoners of war digging the footings for the houses. I can remember jumping over the footings and the prisoners just used to look at us and laugh. One particular day when I was jumping around I lost my red scarf. And the next day when I was passing by one of the prisoners, who had found it and kept it for me, gave it back to me.

Janet Rayner (born 1937)

I Taught Singing and Country Dancing

After a couple of years teaching the infants I asked Mr Richards if I could be the 'floating teacher' because I wanted to move on and teach a different class. And he said that I could because nobody else was keen on doing it anyway. So I ended up doing a lot of the music and helping the children in the lowest group with their reading. I also took country dancing and singing and I really enjoyed that year, after which I started in the junior school. Music lessons involved mainly singing although later on I also taught the recorder. But in those days it was just mainly singing lessons and country dancing. We did have a school choir but this involved mainly the older children which Mr Richards would teach.

Anna Streatfield (born 1933)

Not Everybody in the Choir Was Actually Singing

On one occasion Mr Richards, the headmaster, was developing a choir. He had the class on the stage singing and he was listening to each one sing in turn. And depending upon how good they were he was either saying 'carry on' or 'just mouth the words', and when he got to me, much to my surprise, he said, 'carry on.' So I carried on and then he tapped me on the shoulder quite a lot harder and said, 'No, stop!' He'd changed his mind so I was in the choir mouthing the words, but not singing. So not everybody in the choir at our Christmas play was actually singing.

Steve Bailey (born 1948)

Right: Janet Read aged five.

Left: Anna Streatfield
(formerly Tripp, nee Hedges)
October 2015.

We Used to Sing Ten Green Bottles

When the air raid siren used to go off when I was in the first year infants' class, we used to go out of the classroom, walk down the hall to the corridor between the classrooms and there we would sit and sing songs until the All Clear went. The outside shelters were for the older children but we had to stay in the school. As we got older we would have to go outside and cross the playground to the air raid shelters. We used to go in these shelters and sing songs such as *Ten Green Bottles.* We didn't have lessons as such, it was just something to keep us entertained.

Maureen Ruddock (born 1935)

We Had to Take Our Gas Masks to School

When I was in Miss Hart's class I can remember her taking us down into the air raid shelter. We had to take our gas masks to school and if you forgot to take it you would have to go home and get it. I remember my mum saying to me, 'Now if you hear an aeroplane coming over, very low down, you must lay down against a wall.' I remember that we had to practise what to do if the siren went. We would put our gas masks on and then sit down under our desks, and you would get very hot and you couldn't see anything. That was my earliest memory, but as a rule we went down to the air raid shelter every time the siren went - the whole school. As soon as the siren went off we had to file out and we knew which shelter we had to go in. Our's was the one closest to the church. When we got inside the shelter there was a row of wooden seats along each side and a row down the middle. We would then all sit down and sing songs.

Margaret Moss (born 1934)

I Had to Teach All the Lessons to the Class

I had to teach all the lessons to the class, except for singing which was handled by Miss Hart. At the start of the school day we would all congregate in the hall for a short morning service which was conducted by the headmaster, Mr Hindle. This would usually take the form of a hymn and a short prayer, which I feel was a very good start to the day. And then the children would just disperse into the various classrooms. We would teach Scripture, Maths, Reading and a certain amount of History and Geography. More or less all the subjects that you would teach in schools, but at a lower level. And the children also had to learn their Times Tables. We also did PE in the playground and the boys would have been taken for football, although I can't remember the girls playing netball at that time. I do remember, however, Bobby Hunt, arriving at school everyday with a football under his arm, and they would play football in the playground. He went on to play football for Colchester United.

Mary Holford (born 1920)

It Was My Job to Ring the School Bell

In the old Victorian part of the school the windows were so high that the children couldn't see out of them. There was one big classroom in the school which was always used as the reception class, because it was the biggest classroom of all. And then there were two classrooms which were joined by a partition down the middle, which could be rolled back if necessary but I never saw it happen. And, or course, the school bell hung down in one of those rooms. We rang the school bell every single day and it was my job to ring the bell by hanging on the bell rope. You rang the bell five minutes before school was due to start and the sound of it would echo around Old Heath - which I think used to worry the headmaster at times. And then in between lessons you had to go up and down the corridor ringing a hand bell. This was a job that the children loved to do. And they would say, 'Please can I go and ring the bell?' And then we would ring the school bell again five minutes before the afternoon sessions started. The outside classroom (known as the Hut) was always used for the top class.

Mary Bareham (born 1934)

Old Heath Board School shortly after its construction in 1894.   The Bell Tower in 2015.

The Slipper Was the Usual Form of Punishment

The teachers in general were really strict in those days, but I don't think that you resented it. I remember that we had Mr Green in our last year and he was quite a tough chap, but you certainly learnt your tables. Mr Lishman used to take us for craft subjects and things like that, and also Miss McKeever who again was very strict, but I liked her. The cane was used as a rarity, but the slipper was the more usual form of punishment, which didn't really hurt too much. It was just a case of 'Bend Over' and Whack in front of the class. I remember on one occasion, when we were in the top class, all the boys had lined up in the playground and were dashing from one side to the other, and we did that a few times. As a result of this we all got hauled inside by Mr Richards who proceeded to line us all up in the hall - all of us - and made us bend over and he went down the whole line with his slipper. I suppose that us running across the playground like that was a bit frightening for the younger children.

Stephen Cudmore (born 1947)

Stephen Cudmore, February 2016.

I Remember Feeling Hot With Fear

I can remember the air raid siren going off at school and I have a really vivid memory of the teachers hurrying us through the hall and I can remember feeling really hot with fear. We went across the hall and out the door at the back of the playground. Inside the shelters were a row of low wooden seats which we all sat on, and I remember it smelling damp and being dark. Some of the children used to stop in the school corridors because there wasn't enough room in the shelters. We would sing songs such as *Ten Green Bottles*.

Janet Rayner (born 1937)

We Were Very Successful at Netball

After teaching the infants for some while, Mr Richards, the headmaster, asked if I would like to take the elder girls for sport and games - because he knew that I was keen on that and had played for my college in London, so somebody ended up taking my class for a couple of afternoons a week, while I took the older girls for games. Generally speaking, we had two classes together and played netball in the playground. We soon got a team together and started playing other schools. We also used to practise after school because the games lesson was not long enough to do much, and after school I would run a netball club. There were seven girls in a netball team and during lessons we could have two teams playing each other, and because we had two netball courts all the girls could take part - even if they were not chosen to be in the school team. We were very successful and the team won most things. There was a rally each year and all the schools would send teams in and there was a cup presented to the winners. But for the rest of the time it was just the pride of winning for your school.

Mary Bareham (born 1934)

Teacher, Mary Bareham, with the cup-winning school netball team, 1976.

We Were Allowed to Give the Children a Smack

We were allowed to give the children a smack in those days if they misbehaved, and the cane was still being used, although it had to be noted down in a book. Even then it was only used on rare occasions and it was the headmaster who would do that. We did occasionally use a slipper to discipline a child, and it would take place there and then in front of the other children, who I don't think used to take much notice. But I always believed in giving a child fair warning first.

Anna Streatfield (born 1933)

Above: This group photograph from the year 1969/70 includes both the girls' netball team and the boys' football team, both of whom were successful in their respective competitions. Also included are Miss Bareham, Mr Lishman and Mr Cudmore (right).

Below: Class group from 1961. Note part of the World War II air raid shelter in the background.

We Played Cards and Marbles

We used to play cards and marbles outside at playtime. We used to call them fag cards and you either played to win cards from your friends, or you would swap cards with other people so you could make a set up. There were different collections that you could save. Popular during my time at school were Brook Bond Tea cards where you could make up a number of different sets. One of the games that we used to play to win cards was where you would stand some cards up against a wall, at an angle, and then you had to flick your card from some distance away and try to knock those cards down. If your card didn't hit a card, or didn't knock it over, it was the next person's go. And whoever managed to knock the last card over had all of those on the deck.

Steve Bailey (born 1948)

Above: A class group from 1956.

Below: The teaching staff pictured sometime in the 1970s.

Steve Bailey aged 11.

Class group from 1953/54.

Chapter Three

Church & Chapel

We Used to Go to the Seaside With the Church

Once a year we used to go to the seaside with the church and we had to pay sixpence (2½p). We had to pay sixpence each to go to Clacton. We used to go by train from St Botolph's Station and we used to have sixpence pocket money to take with us for the day, and I remember that we used to spend nearly all of it in the chocolate machines at St Botolph's Station. You would put a penny in and get a bar of chocolate out. Sometimes dad would drive us down to Mersea in his pony and cart, and my brother and I used to go exploring around the oyster beds.

Fred Johnson (born 1902)

St Barnabas' Church, c.1930.

Old Heath Congregational Church in 2005.

Sunday Was a Special Day

Sunday was a special day. We used to go to chapel every Sunday morning, and Sunday school in the afternoons. And then to service again in the evening. We had to wear our Sunday best which included little white gloves. There used to be an anniversary once a year when we would go to Lion Walk Church. Mr Webb would sometimes come to the chapel to preach on Sundays. Several people would come and take it in turns to preach - we didn't have a permanent preacher. Quite a few children used to attend Sunday school in the afternoon. Miss Rose used to play the organ and she also took a class. Her sister Lilian would also take a class. Once a year we would go to the anniversary at Lion Walk Church where all the different Sunday schools would meet up. After chapel on a Sunday evening, if it was nice, we used to go for a walk with father and mother. We would go down by Place Farm, along the riverbank to Rowhedge, and up the road home.

Flossie Lappage (born 1905)

Sundays Were Mostly Spent at the Congregational Chapel

Sundays were mostly spent at the Congregational Chapel. We went in the mornings and would come out about midday. Us boys would then go over the Wick for a couple of hours before dinner. After we had eaten our dinner it was back to Sunday school in the afternoon, and then again in the evening. It was a duty and we had to go - and we had no excuse to get out of it. Father never used to attend, but mother would go in the afternoon and take a class - she was very religious. There was quite a little gathering that went to the chapel at Old Heath. Sometimes we would have a change and go to church for six months, and then back to the chapel. Most of the children went to church or chapel, at least once during the day.

Bob Allen (born 1906)

We Had to Say Grace Before Eating

Sunday was a very special day. Mother made us all a nice white apron to wear in the shop. It went over our shoulder and was tied round our waist. We had to keep that on all day because we had our best Sunday suits on. And when sitting round the table everything had to be just so before mother would start serving out the meals. No argument - any arguments - nothing to eat. And we always had to say grace before we started eating - if not you got a clip round the ear. None of you had anything until you had all said it. And we were not allowed to talk at mealtimes - not a word - it was like being in a monastery.

Steve Mason (born 1906)

The Summers Seemed So Much Hotter Then

We used to go on Sunday school outings to Clacton by train. We would walk from Old Heath to the Hythe, and the train fare was ninepence (3½p). My mother used to come and four or five from the family. The summers seemed so much hotter then and you roasted in your suit, which was made for the winter. We paddled in the sea and would go on the pier, but there were no amusements like you have today.

Bob Allen (born 1906)

My Father Was a Very Religious Man

We never did any work on Sundays. My father, Alfred Crick, was a very religious man and we had to go to chapel - perhaps three times on a Sunday. Morning service at eleven o'clock, three o'clock Sunday school and half past six for the evening service. My father used to go round preaching - sometimes at Old Heath, or perhaps at the Hythe, and occasionally the Minister from Lion Walk Church - the Reverend Parrott, or Owen Ward, from the outfitters shop in town, would come round. My father had never received any special training for preaching - if he had been an educated man he would have gone very far. He knew his Bible very well.

Les Crick (born 1906)

Les Crick (seated) alongside his mother Jane and father Alfred, with other members of the Crick family.

He Was a Real Hell Raiser
We didn't dare do anything on a Sunday and we had to wear our Sunday best. We couldn't even sew or knit on a Sunday. As little girls we used to go to the Congregational Chapel for the eleven o'clock service in the morning. Then we would go home for dinner, change our clothes in case they were messed up, and then back again to Sunday school in the afternoon. And then it was back to a service again in the evening. In those days they used to have a lay preacher at the chapel, one in the morning and another in the evening. One of the preachers was a man called Victor Bland who came from the Harwich area. He used to shout quite loudly - a real hell-raiser. In the summer the chapel door used to be left open and they could hear him preaching over at Mason's shop. They used to say, 'Old Victor is holding forth, listen.'

Phyllis Gibbins (born 1915)

Phyllis Gibbins, aged eighteen.

We Thought That the Better People Went to Church
Sunday was a special day. We went to Sunday school and chapel, and although father didn't go, he would always put his best suit on. He would look at the garden, but he wouldn't use a spade on it. And us children were not allowed to play outside on a Sunday. We went to chapel at eleven o'clock in the morning for the service, and then in the afternoon we would go to Sunday school. Our Sunday school teachers were Hilda and Stella Rowe. The congregation was larger than it is today. We always thought that the people who went to St Barnabas' Church were higher than those who went to chapel - we thought the better people went to church and the poorer people went to chapel.

Edna Mills (born 1918)

We Always had to Wear Our Sunday Best
I always used to go to Sunday school at St Barnabas' Church with my brother. Beryl Bones used to be our Sunday school teacher, and as we got a little older we used to have a Bible class. Later on during the war years, after I had been evacuated, I started going to the little chapel by the side of the Bell public house. It was a smaller congregation and I later got married in Lion Walk Church, which was the mother church to Old Heath Congregational Chapel. We always had to wear our Sunday best clothes and at Easter time we used to make our own dresses. I can also remember on one occasion during the war years we put on a little concert for the older people.

Gladys Rudd (born 1927)

Gladys Rudd (seated centre), aged eighteen, with her parents and brother and sister, c.1945.

We Sat on the Lawn at the Vicarage Singing Songs

We were not allowed to play out in the street on a Sunday. We had to stay in the garden and we always went to Sunday school at St Barnabas' Church in the afternoon. Our parents were not regular churchgoers, but us children always had to go to Sunday school. We used to meet in the church itself and I can remember the Reverend and Mrs Brooksbank, who I think were missionaries in China at one stage. And I can remember on one occasion sitting on the front lawn at the old Vicarage, next to where the current one is, and singing a song called '*Jesus wants me for a Sunbeam*', and accompanied by a harmonium. I can also recall sitting in the church at Harvest Festival time and looking round the church because you would be absolutely surrounded by flowers, fruit and vegetables. You actually felt quite small because everything was towering over you. Everywhere was piled high with sheaves of corn and there was a lovely smell to it all.

Janet Rayner (born 1937)

People Used to Sit in Their Own Regular Pews

On Sundays we all used to go to St Barnabas' Church. This was in the old church and I can remember that different families used to have their own regular pews. We always went to the evening service and nine times out of ten I used to go to sleep during the sermon because I was tired. We never went to church in the morning because all the animals had to be attended to. We also used to attend Sunday school and the teachers were Daisy Norfolk and Connie Coe. This used to take place in the church hall, and then for the last part of the class we used to have to go into the church.

Janet Read (born 1945)

Our Parents Made Us Go to Church

My parents didn't worry at all about Sundays because we had a shop to keep and you couldn't stop work on Sundays. The shop was always open on a Sunday - it never closed. However, our parents made us go to St Barnabas' Church because they were very strict on good living. We would generally go to church in the afternoon, and sometimes in the evening if there was anything special on. There used to be an old parson there that we used to call 'Old Daddy White'. He was a big fellow about seven feet tall and was built like a boxer. He was a powerful man with snow-white hair and a beard - so we used to call him 'Snowy'. If you did anything wrong or giggled, you would have a prayer book flung at you. You had to keep quiet.

Steve Mason (born 1906)

Keith Moss, aged eleven in 1945.

We Had to Stick Stamps into a Little Book

My sister and I used to go to Sunday school at St Barnabas' Church. This was on a Sunday afternoon and I can remember that we had to stick these stamps into a book so we knew how many times we had attended. We used to play a few games to start with and would then go into the church for a little singsong and then home. We had to get dressed up for that in our Sunday best - these were clothes that we wouldn't normally wear during week.

Keith Moss (born 1934)

St Barnabas' Church and Church Hall, c.1940.

St Barnabas' Church Choir, February 2014.

I Had Never Been in a Choir Before

I became a member of St Barnabas' Church choir in 1974 and I'd never previously been in a choir. We had about fourteen in the choir to begin with and we had to attend choir practice religiously every week. This was in the evenings usually in the church hall - I think that we found it warmer in there and there was a piano in there as well. But nowadays, of course, we do it in the church. To begin with our choir master was Mrs Green and after she died we had Mr Sparkes. On Sundays we would attend morning service and sometimes again in the evening. It was a mixed choir with men and ladies. I did find it quite difficult at times as some choir masters were a little more strict that others. I think I probably know most of the hymns inside out by now, but we no longer sing the Psalms like we used to as they are now included as part of the readings.

Maureen Gooding (born 1931)

Maureen and Frank Gooding, pictured together in February 2016.

Chapter Four

Wartime

Middlewick Was Full of Tents

During the First World War Middlewick was full of tents - it was covered from top to bottom with tents. My brother Cyril and I used to come out of school and go and get about a peck (10 pounds) of apples each and then go over the Wick and sell these apples for a ha'penny for the small ones, and a penny for the big ones. And sometimes we'd see a Redcap come racing across towards us on horseback and he'd say, 'Don't you come over here any more', so we would just jump over to the other side of the hedge, but as soon as he was gone we'd be back over the hedge selling our apples.

Fred Johnson (born 1902)

Fred Johnson, c.1970.

There Used to be Lots of Horses on the Wick

During the First World War there used to be lots of horses on the Wick. I remember going to School one day and suddenly coming upon fifty or so horses with soldiers. The horses used to kick and would sometimes break loose, and the children got really frightened. I remember on one occasion walking up to Recreation Road and seeing these two mules with these young soldiers, and they were having trouble making them go forward and they were really thrashing them. They used to train the horses on the Wick and they were all tethered up there. When I was young my father used to take me up there to see them.

Flossie Lappage (born 1905)

We Used to Have to Queue For Our Rations

Food was rationed during the First World War. I remember on one occasion having to queue at the Maypole in Long Wyre Street for our butter. It was quite a hot day and by the time I had got to the Recreation Ground on the way home, the butter was melting. So I asked some soldiers who were passing in a horse and cart if they would take my butter home for me. There was no money to buy any more. We also had a couple of soldiers plonked on us during the war with their blankets and they slept downstairs in the front room. The field on the Wick was full of army tents, and the field beyond it. There were also loads of horses there all roped together.

Bob Allen (born 1906)

We Heard This Zeppelin Come Over One Night

When the First World War came along we were used to seeing many soldiers around here because they used to have an army camp on the Middlewick. They all wore coloured uniforms when you saw them in the streets. I can remember the first bombs being dropped in the Butt Road area and then, of course, the next thing was the zeppelins coming over. At night time you couldn't have a light shining, and your blinds had to be tight shut. One night we heard this zeppelin coming over and we were all in darkness. We crept out of the house and walked up the yard and this zeppelin came over and shortly after we heard the bombing and it dropped some bombs on the site of the Lathe Company, and also damaged a few houses in Greenstead Road. Many of the troops in the town were billeted on the various houses, and I remember that we had several lots of soldiers billeted with us. There was also a big camp just outside of Old Heath on the Military Road which was run by the Royal Army Medical Corps who used to put on various concert parties, and we would go up there sometimes and see them as boys and girls.

Les Crick (born 1906)

I Remember the Zeppelin Coming Down at Wigborough

I remember the zeppelin coming down at Wigborough. I wanted to go and see it but my mother said that I wasn't to go. But I really wanted to go so I went on my bike with my father to see it. There were crowds of people there and the roads were packed, and I only came off my bike once on the way back. It was just a huge metal frame lying in the field.

Flossie Lappage (born 1905)

Soldiers camped near Old Heath

We Had to Black Out All Our Windows
We were living at 1 D'arcy Road when the Second World War started. We had an Anderson shelter in the garden which we put up ourselves, although nine times out of ten when there was an air raid on we all just used to just go under the stairs. We had to black out all of our windows - you were not allowed to have a light anywhere. There used to be an Air Raid Warden on each street who would come round to check if any light was showing. He also provided us with a gas mask each. The baby had a special one - we used to lay her right in that. Our Air Raid Warden was Mr Beales and I remember him coming along and showing us what to do.

Albert Bridges (born 1908)

A Siren Went Off and We Really Got the Jitters
I can remember the war starting when it was given out on 3 September 1939. A siren went off soon after and we really got the jitters. We thought that it had started right away. We had a public shelter at the bottom of our garden which was used by all the people in the four cottages. At the beginning of the war we used to get up every time there was a raid on, but after a while we would stay where we were until the All Clear went.

Edna Mills (born 1918)

I Thought the Plane Was Going to Hit the Houses
I remember standing in our garden at Canwick Grove when war was declared on a Sunday morning - it was given out on the wireless. It didn't worry us too much at the time because we didn't know what was coming. We didn't think that it was going to last for six years My husband built a shelter in the garden, underground with seats all round. The people next door, about five of them, would also come in sometimes. I can remember the raid on the Chapel Street area - I saw that plane go over and thought it was going to hit the houses in Cavendish Avenue, because it was flying so low that I could see the markings on it. I didn't realise that it was a German plane at the time, until I heard the bombs.

Daisy Haines (born 1911)

We Wore a Siren Suit to Go in the Shelter
We moved to Cavendish Avenue in 1940. The war was on and we built an Anderson shelter in the garden. When the siren went we used to go to the shelter dressed in a one-piece 'Siren Suit'. We had blackout blinds in the front of the house, and my husband Fred made shutters for the back. He also had to go to the Home Guard twice a week after working to about eight at night. When he got home from work it was straight to the Home Guard without any sleep, and then it was work the next morning.

Eileen Humphrey (born 1915)

Daisy Haines.

We Are Now at War With Germany

I had only been married a month when we heard the announcement on the radio one Sunday morning that, 'We are now at war with Germany'. My heart sank in my boots, despite the fact that we'd been more or less expecting it. The most serious raid that I can remember is the Chapel Street one. I was standing at my kitchen window in Barn Hall Avenue, where we were living then, and I saw this big bomber with a Swastika on it, and it was flying very low over the back of the houses in Cavendish Avenue. I pushed the children into the shelter and then went to the front door to see if I could still see the plane, and just as I shut the front door I heard the explosion.

Phyllis Gibbins (born 1915)

People Were Starting to Get Quite Worried

At the time of the Second World War my husband and I were living in Canwick Grove. About a fortnight before war was declared we were staying down at Brightlingsea where we had a hut. I remember that people were starting to get quite worried then, but my husband said not to worry as it wouldn't start for another week or two. When we came home my husband went up the garden and said that he was going to dig a shelter, so he started digging and the man next door said that he would also dig from his side. When it was finished we had steps leading down into it.

Doris Thimblethorpe (born 1903)

Several Fire Bombs Were Dropped in Old Heath

On one occasion we had several fire bombs drop within 100 yards of where we live in Old Heath. You could see the planes coming over and see them setting their markers out. Fortunately, the bombs fell in the fields and a sandpit - but it made a big blaze. Fire-fighters were chaining buckets of water all the way up the fields and put out as much as they could.

Les Crick (born 1906)

The Hedges All Caught Alight

I remember when they dropped the incendiary bombs in Old Heath about eight o'clock one evening and all the hedges caught alight. My son was in his cot at the time under a big oak table. Lots of local people went and helped. They had pails of water and were trying to put the fires out in case the bombers returned to drop some more bombs after having lit the area up. The whole area was ablaze and it lit the sky up.

Emily Tricker (born 1906)

We Spent Most of the Night Putting the Fires Out

We had an enemy plane come over one night. I was on my way down Whitehall Road to the Malsters public house to have a drink with a mate of mine and we saw this plane come over which dropped a basket full of incendiaries - it was a big basket full of lights and it was gradually coming down on a parachute. And I said to my mate, 'Look out', and I pushed him into a ditch, with me following right behind him straight into some stinging nettles. And there was a line of these incendiaries which landed right in the middle of the road, and we just managed to get out of the way in time. There was no end of these little incendiary fires up Whitehall Road and I went round with a shovel to help put them out - there were little old sheds burning all over the place. The fires spread all round the orchard and round my brother's chicken sheds, and all the hedges were alight. We spent most of the night putting the fires out, but thankfully nobody got hurt. And I can remember at about twelve o'clock that night I went and knocked on the door of Jerry Martin's off-licence and got a bottle of ale - he was still up.

Fred Johnson (born 1902)

Phyllis and Harold Gibbins pictured at the seaside in the late 1930s.

I Used To Watch the Doodlebugs Flying Over

During the war I used to do a paper round for Mr Claydon, who had the Post Office at Old Heath, opposite Cavendish Avenue. And that paper round took me down to Distillery Lane and then up to Fingringhoe Road. And I can often remember seeing doodlebugs coming over while I was doing my round, and I would stop and watch them flying overhead. I can also remember the time when a massive bomb dropped at the back of our house in Speedwell Road, showering the house all over with debris.

John Hedges (born 1931)

John Hedges.

We Had a Big Air Raid Shelter at the Bottom of Our Garden

We had quite a long back garden at 133 Old Heath Road which included a lovely big air raid shelter at the bottom of the garden. You went down the steps and turned right and there were some bunk beds on the left side and some more on the other side. And we had duck boards on the floor. And I remember in 1940, when all the planes were going over to London, we slept in there every night. We had a Hurricane lamp in there and mum used to take some food in, and we would stay down there until seven o'clock in the morning. And then we'd come up and go to school. Several of our neighbours who lived nearby used to come down there with us.

Margaret Moss (born 1934)

Margaret Moss, November 2015.

Below: The present occupants of 133 Old Heath Road, Gayna and David Gabriel, standing on what was once the roof of the old underground air raid shelter at the back of the home.

Everybody had a Gas Mask

I was twelve years old when war broke out and I can remember lying in bed one night with mum and seeing this plane in the sky with all its lights on. And I said to my mum, 'Mum, that plane has got all its fairy lights on.' So she said, 'Don't be silly, it hasn't got any fairy lights on.' And the next morning we found out that it was a German plane on fire and it crashed at Wivenhoe. I can also remember cycling to school one day and getting my gas mask caught in the wheel of my bike. They came round the house to issue you with your gas mask and everybody had to have one. And when you went out you had to take it with you - wherever you went.

Gladys Rudd (born 1927)

They Brought the Gas Masks Round in a Suitcase

I was at home when I heard that war had been declared. And after that all the men around where I lived decided that they were going to build a shelter. So they went out to this field behind our house and dug a hole to make a shelter. We were issued with a gas mask, and I remember that they came round to the house with a big suitcase with all these gas masks in, and they measured you up for your mask. I think that there were three sizes - small, medium and large, but I wouldn't let them put one on me. I wasn't going to put my face into that. It took me a long while before I would put it on. I was afraid that I wouldn't be able to breathe.

Frank Gooding (born 1931)

We Had To Have Our Gas Masks Checked

On one occasion my mum sent my sister Barbara and I up to the ARP (Air Raid Precautions) Station in Whitehall Road to have our gas masks checked. They had this van there to test your gas mask to check that it was alright. I was a bit of a tomboy at the time and my gas mask had hit the wall on a few occasions and I knew that the end of it was all dented in. And I remember standing there with my sister and thinking that I was going to die. Because someone had said that they turn the gas on and you have to walk through the van wearing your mask and come out the other end. And I remember thinking, ' I'm going, I'm not staying here.' And I did, I ran all the way down Whitehall Road and my sister was chasing after me saying, 'You'll get it, what will mum say?' I said, 'I don't care what mum will say, I'm not going to die.' So I never did have it tested. And I don't think that my sister had hers tested either.

Margaret Moss (born 1934)

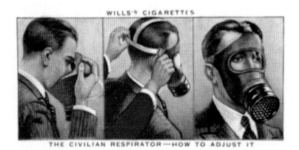

A Will's cigarette card giving instructions on how to put on your gas mask.

Frank Gooding, February 2016

We Slept in the Bathroom When There Was a Raid On
When the war started and before the shelters came, we used to sleep in the bathroom because it was a downstairs room off the kitchen. My brother slept in the bath and my sister and I had a mattress on the floor. Later on we had one of those table shelters in the living room. We didn't actually sleep in it, but if there was a bad raid on we were taken downstairs and put underneath. At other times we would sometimes play table tennis on it.

Joy Cardy (born 1934)

Above left: Entrance to a surviving underground air raid shelter in a Colchester garden.

Above right: Interior view of shelter, most of which is buried underground. Floor space approx. 6 ft x 4 ft.

We Hadn't Got a Clue Where We Were Going
In September 1940 I was evacuated. I went with my younger brother Albert (aged 10) and sister Flo (aged 7), and I can remember mum and dad coming down to the station to see us off at ten o'clock in the morning. And it was one o'clock the next morning when we got to where we were going. We hadn't got a clue where we were going. We just sat in the train and we were shunted backwards and forwards. It was stop and go all the time. And we didn't have a clue where we were because all the names of the stations had been blacked out. When we got up there [Stoke on Trent] they herded us all into a church hall. We were all stripped and washed and there was a 'nit nurse' to make sure that nobody had anything wrong with them, and then we were given something to eat and drink. And then we were like cattle. We had to stand and wait to be picked out by all these men and women.

Gladys Rudd (born 1927)

There Were Mothers and Children All Over the Place
I was evacuated along with my mother and brother in 1940. We were taken to North Station and put on a train which took us to Stoke-on-Trent. And when we got there we were taken to a huge hall where there were mothers and children all over the place, and I can see it now as if it were

yesterday. And that's where we spent the night. Everyone had to go in front of the doctor and we were the last ones to be seen, and he said to my mother, ' I don't know where you've come from, but you are among the healthiest children that I've seen.' The next morning we were taken out in parties, knocking on doors and asking, 'How many can you take?' And eventually we were taken in by a woman (whose husband had died), and her son, who only cooked food at a weekend and lived off it for the rest of the week. She was very house proud and everything had to be just so. My mother used to walk the streets during the day, or go for a walk over the park, just to get out of it.

Keith Pettit (born 1934)

Left: Gladys Rudd, November 2015.

Below: Keith Pettit (centre) with younger brothers David (left) and Michael (right), c.1950.

All of Us Children Were Put On a Train

I can remember one day seeing my mother crying and I couldn't understand what was wrong. My nan had called round which was unusual and the next thing I knew we were on the bus going to North Station. All of us children were then put on a train, and I can remember crying and wanting to get off, and my mother saying, 'No, you've got to go.' I didn't realise at the time that I was being evacuated. The first place that I was sent to was a place in Wellington, Shropshire and it was terrible. I was staying there with a girl and I can remember being there for a few weeks before I was moved. Suddenly, this lady appeared and we were both moved and I ended up on the doorstep of a house where the lady who lived there was saying that she didn't want to take me in. There was another lady, however, who was in the house and who was listening to this conversation going on, who then said, 'If you take him tonight, I will take him after that.' And, apart from my own parents, that was the best thing that ever happened to me. Their names were Annie and Richard Parker. So I stayed with them and they had chickens, ducks and pigs and a huge garden full of vegetables. They were fantastic people and we kept in touch with them for many years afterwards.

Dick Jackson (born 1937)

Left: Dick Jackson, pictured in 1951 aged 14.

Below: Part of an urgent notice issued to the people of Colchester on 15 September 1940.

URGENT.

Temporary Transfer of Population

The Government and Local Authority are extremely concerned that in response to the warning given on behalf of the Minister of Home Security by the Regional Commissioner (Sir Will Spens) comparatively so few people have taken advantage of the arrangements made for the transfer by special trains of certain classes of the Civil population of the **BOROUGH** and in particular that so many school children are still left in the town.

If invasion takes place on the Essex coast there is a very grave risk that **THIS TOWN** will be heavily bombed.

He Dived Behind the Wall as the Bombs Fell

I remember when they dropped the bombs on the Old Heath Road, and then Scarletts Road and then the Laundry. It was lunch time and we were at home under the stairs when it happened. The siren had sounded and my father had come home for his lunch and he was cycling back up Cannock Hill when it happened. And when he got to the top of the hill, near Winsley's Square, he dived down behind a wall as the bombs fell. At the same time one of our neighbours who lived opposite to us was passing the other way and my father asked him if he would nip in and tell my mother that he was alright.

Frank Gooding (born 1931)

I Remember the Day That Old Heath Laundry Got Hit

I remember the day that Old Heath Laundry got hit - I can remember it as clear as if it was yesterday. My father used to go down and cycle along Distillery Lane and round the pond to Brackett's where he worked. He used to leave home at one o'clock sharp after dinner to get back in time for work. And on this particular day the siren went at one o'clock and he said, 'I'm off.' and my mum said, 'Please don't go Jack, please hold on.' And he said, 'Oh, alright then.' And within four or five minutes there were these almighty bangs. They had hit the laundry - another one went in the pond and one hit a house in Scarlett's Road, where that lad and his mum were just going back to school. They were coming out of their front door when the bomb hit and they were killed. Another one fell on Old Heath Hill and one landed in somebody's kitchen on Old Heath Road. And I can remember our windows - how they didn't break - the vibration was terrible. My mother was on the floor with a kettle of boiling water in her hand because we got down. She was trying to get us into the air raid shelter and she was crawling around with this kettle of boiling water. That did frighten me.

Margaret Moss (born 1934)

This German Bomber Came Right Out of the Clouds

My friend and I were walking down Old Heath Road on the day that the Laundry got bombed. We had got as far as the youth hut on the corner of D'arcy Road when this German bomber came right out of the clouds. And Mr Langley, who owned the nearby butcher's shop, ran across the road and grabbed my friend and I and took us over into his shop. This was the plane that went on to drop his load on Old Heath Laundry where I think a number of girls were killed. I remember later going to see the damage - if anything was happening during the war, we were there to see it.

John Hedges (born 1931)

Margaret Moss, aged twelve in 1946.

Above: Old Heath Laundry as seen in 1930.

Below: Old Heath Laundry after it had been destroyed by enemy bombing on 3 October 1939.

I Was in My Cot When the Plane Came Over

I think it was sometime during the early part of 1942 when an enemy plane came over and machine-gunned the houses in Scarletts Road. I was in my cot at the time and my mother was talking to a neighbour over the garden fence when she heard the plane coming over. She just had time to rush upstairs, grab me out of my cot, and then downstairs again before diving into the Morrison shelter as the house got hit. Her father, who had been standing at the top of his garden nearby and saw what had happened, came running round and when he went upstairs he found that where I'd been lying a bullet had gone right through the cot. And I had this bullet, which my grandfather had retrieved, with me until I lost it about 10 years ago. I'd kept it as a souvenir.

Barri Clements (born 1941)

The Milkman Used to Deliver Rabbits

Food was very tight during the war and because my mother had three children she wasn't able to get into Colchester. The milkman used to bring rabbits round and we were very lucky that we had Johnson's, a sort of market gardener, opposite the school, where we could buy vegetables. The children would buy carrots from them on the way to school, scrape off the skins as they went along, wash them in the basins at school, and then have them to eat instead of sweets. We would also go and buy things like blackcurrants and redcurrants and things like that. They would sell us a pennyworth.

Joy Cardy (born 1934)

The remains of two houses in Scarletts Road which were destroyed by enemy bombing in October 1940. Two of the occupants, Mrs Ethel Strong and her five year son Bernard, both received fatal injuries.

We Hadn't Had Oranges for Years
One day during the war I was walking home from school past Humphrey's, the greengrocers, [now Burgess] and I saw that there was a big queue forming and someone said that they have got oranges, and we hadn't had any oranges for years. And I ran all the way home and told my mum about these oranges and she hurried up there and got in the queue - and they were allowed two oranges each. So we had an orange - but we never saw a banana. We didn't know what a banana looked like until after the war.

Margaret Moss (born 1934)

It Looked Like the Whole of Colchester Was Ablaze
One night I looked out of my bedroom window in Speedwell Road and saw what appeared to be the whole of Colchester ablaze. This was the night when St Botolph's Corner got hit and we could see the glow, so we knew something had happened. I went to see it the next morning. I should have been at school, of course, but like many other children I never went that morning. When we got down to St Botolph's Station it was absolute chaos with hose pipes laying around and water running everywhere. We had a little sand bag each and we went round picking up bits and pieces which we put in our sand bags and took them home. We then spent the rest of the day cleaning them up with Vim in the sink and trying to get all the black off. You wouldn't get away with it today.

John Hedges (born 1931)

There Was a Fireball in the Sky
I can remember my father waking me up and taking me to the bedroom window and there was a fireball in the sky, and I think that it was the night when there was a bombing raid on St Botolph's Corner. There was just this great big glow in the sky.

Tony Gibbins (born 1940)

The aftermath of the devastating raid on St Botolph's Corner in February 1944. The tower of St Botolph's Church is partly visible through the smoking ruins.

Tony Gibbins, aged seven in 1947.

The Sky Was Red With Flames
The one night that I do remember was when they hit St Botolph's Corner. Mum got us up and we stood on the garden seat and it looked as though the whole of Colchester was on fire. I'd never seen anything like it - the sky was red with flames. And the next day it was awful. Hollingtons, the clothing factory, was gone and all those shops around St Botolph's Corner - they were all burnt out. I remember thinking how terrible it was, but we just had to get on with it - you just took it in your stride.

Margaret Moss (born 1934)

An Incendiary Bomb Landed in a Wardrobe
I was working in the coupon office at Hollingtons when it was destroyed in the bombing raid on St Botolph's Corner. The next morning we went into town to see what we had to do because we didn't have any jobs. We were told to go home while they decided what to do with us and I ended up being transferred to their London office. And it was while I was working up there that the first doodlebugs were dropped. The scene around St Botolph's Corner was just a mess and rubble. The shop where my dad worked [Blomfield's] had gone. My father-in-law, who lived in Osborne Street, was an air raid warden and during the raid an incendiary had been dropped on a house in Arthur Street and had gone right through the roof and landed in a wardrobe - and he had to go in and put it out.

Gladys Rudd (born 1927)

We Were Invited to the VE Day Celebrations
When the war came to an end we were all invited to the VE Day Celebrations. Many of the children first congregated in Canwick Grove where they took part in a fancy dress parade. My mother, who was a good dressmaker made me a paper dress. She bought these strips of coloured paper from a little printing shop in Old Heath Road [now 235 Old Heath Road] and she stitched all these pieces together and turned them into a frock for me to wear. She also made me a bonnet and named the costume, 'Coupon Free'. And I got first prize for that - or rather my mother did! After the fancy dress parade we went into Cavendish Avenue where there were loads of trestle tables set up in the centre of the road where we sat down to eat our cakes and jellies. There must have been hundreds of children there and every family gave something towards the tea. After that was all over we all marched over to the Wick where we had fun and games.

Maureen Ruddock (born 1935)

This group photograph was taken on the Wick following some of the local VE Day celebrations

Maureen Ruddock, aged eleven.

Joy Cardy.

We Had a Street Party With Tables Full of Food
When the war finished we had street parties to celebrate. Our street party was at the junction of Wick Road and Speedwell Road, with tables full of food. We had games and races afterwards and that kind of thing.

Joy Cardy (born 1934)

We Went Crazy When the War Ended
When the war ended we nearly went crazy. We had a street party in Cavendish Avenue with tables set up down the centre of the road. They were laid out with everything that we could get - cakes, biscuits and sandwiches. We had a really good do.

Daisy Haines (born 1911)

There Was an Enormous Bonfire Over the Wick
We were invited to an end of war street party in Cavendish Avenue. We all sat down at long tables down the middle of the road, and our parents and neighbours provided all the food. I can remember the music being played opposite where Canwick Grove is, and in the evening they lit this enormous bonfire over the Wick. And someone took a wind-up gramophone and all the parents came along and danced around the field.

Margaret Moss (born 1934)

Children line up in their fancy dress costumes at an end of war street party in Canwick Grove in 1945. Maureen Ruddock (nee Bridges) can be seen wearing her paper dress and bonnet just to the left of centre in the front row.

This end of war street party was a joint effort for the residents of both Foresight Road and Speedwell Road.

Above: Local civil defence volunteers practising first aid and fire prevention skills in the school playground. Les Crick can be seen standing to the left of the picture.

Below: The full line up of the Old Heath Civil Defence Group pictured in the school playground.

Chapter Five

Occupation and Trade

The Coalman Used to Come With His Horse and Cart
There used to be a little pond alongside the Old Heath Road which was fed by a spring in the meadow near the Bell pub. The water used to run into a little structure by the side of the road and would then run out of a spout in the side and down into the pond. It was lovely spring water and people from Old Heath used to go down there with a pail and get the water. They always swore that it was good for their eyes. And I can remember when Mr Osborne, the coalman, who lived in King Stephen Road, used to come along there to Rowhedge twice a day and he used to call out, 'Coalie, Coalie, Coalie, tuppence a hundredweight.' And when he came home from Rowhedge when he was empty he always used to go through the shallow pond with his horse, so it could have a drink and cool its feet.

Fred Johnson (born 1902)

Old Heath Road looking up towards where the Bell public house used to be. The little roadside structure with water pouring out can be seen on the right of the road, just before where the present day junction of Speedwell Road is located, c.1935.

The Doctor Used to Come in a Pony and Trap

Our doctor used to come from Rowhedge in a pony and trap. He had a bell on his pony and a little dog, so you could always hear his bell. The pony would just stand and wait for him, but the little dog would run upstairs in front of him. We had to go to Rowhedge if ever we wanted to attend his surgery. I remember that he was very keen on yachting and when he died his coffin was put onto a yacht and he was taken out to sea.

Flossie Lappage (born 1905)

The Horse-drawn Royal Mail Van Used to Call Every Night

There used to be a Post Office opposite the Bell and the horse-drawn Royal Mail van used to stop here on the way from Mersea at nine o'clock every night. Mason's shop was where the garage is now and they sold cycles and sweets. They were the only shops until you got down to below where the brewery used to be. That was Martin's [later Phillips] which was a small shop and off-licence. Old Heath was separated from Colchester in those days. There was an avenue of trees that went up to Whitehall Road from Cannock Mill, and there was just a single gas lamp along there and that was sometimes alight if the wind was not too strong.

Bob Allen (born 1906)

We Would Be Watching Out for Horse Manure for the Garden

Pocket money was very scant in those days, but there were ways of picking up a copper or two. There were plenty of horses up and down the road so when a horse and cart came along, the boys would be watching for the horse to leave some manure for father's garden. Another regular job was having to clean the knives and forks. We used to clean them with brick dust and would get tuppence or thrupence a week for doing that.

Les Crick (born 1906)

In times past, Cannock Hill was covered with overhanging elm trees which gave the impression that one was entering the countryside as you approached Old Heath from Colchester. As can be seen from the above photograph, some of these trees had recently been felled prior to house building in the early 1930s.

I Earned Two Shillings a Week

We never got any pocket money - not a cent! I never got paid any pocket money until I had left school and started working in my dad's shop. He paid me the massive sum of two shillings a week and he said, 'I'll buy your clothes boy.' My dad's first shop was at Old Heath, the next one was at 70 Maldon Road and then another at 91 Crouch Street. I just has to sit in the shop and wait for customers to come in. We used to do cycle repairs and punctures, and also strip down cycles to the frame before rebuilding them. We would rub down the cycle frames and then repaint them with a paint called 'Rovolac'. It was beautiful stuff to put on with a brush. Then you built them up again and sold them for a good price. Cycles in those days used to be anything up to £30 each.

Steve Mason (born 1906)

Mason's Sold All Sorts of Things

Mason's shop had a wooden place built onto the front of the house, which had a window with sweets in. They sold all sorts of things and inside the shop, to the right, there were bicycles for sale, and a place where punctures and repairs were carried out. They also had some slot machines in there and the little balls would fly round. And if you were lucky, you might get a little money out.

Phyllis Gibbins (born 1915)

Below: Mason's Store as rebuilt about 1930,

I Used to Drive Pigs to the Market

My father kept about 700 pigs at Cockwatch Farm. He used to keep them for various people and he was paid a shilling (5p) a week to keep each pig until it was fat enough to go to market. And when they were ready to go we used to drive them down to North Station. And I've driven 80-100 pigs on my own. We used to go along the Old Heath Road to town, up St Botolph's Street, cross over to Maidenburgh Street, along St Peter's Street, on to North Station Road and right on to North Station. It was easier driving that lot as it was for just six.

Fred Johnson (born 1902)

It Was a Smelly Old Job
My father got me a job at Wambach's down Haven Road, and it was a smelly old job. There was a concrete floor and the place was full of barrels with their tops off. The intestines of bullocks, sheep and pigs were put into the barrels and soaked for about three days until they were soft and could be cleaned out. They were then run through a machine which cleaned the flesh. It was just the guts that were there and it was known as the 'Gut Factory'. All the rubbish was boiled up in a metal digester, and the fat was bagged up like lard, nothing was wasted. The skins became sausage skins. Sheep were for the small ones and pigs for the pork ones. The bullocks were for the German sausages.

Bob Allen (born 1906)

There Used to be a Lot of Sand and Gravel Workings in Old Heath
When I was a lad I we lived at 210 Old Heath Road, opposite the Whitehall Estate. A little way up the old Whitehall Road [now Whitehall Close] there used to be an entry on the right to a sand pit which was owned by Wright & Sons of Greenstead Road. I can remember there being a huge hole there where they were digging out the sand and gravel, which at that time of day was all pick and shovel work, and they had a large sieve, about eight feet high, that they used to throw the gravel into so as to sift the stone from the sand. They would dig the sand out from the edge of the pit and where it fell to the bottom they would load it into their wheelbarrows. They would then run them along wooden planks, which had been laid down, across to the sieve. There would usually be two men working on the pit at one time.

Les Crick (born 1906)

I Got Paid Ninepence a Week
We used to get our milk from Place Farm. We would get it in the mornings, but if mother was short we would go over in the afternoon. We got the milk in a jug and it cost thrupence a pint (1p). I used to earn some pocket money for delivering some milk from Place Farm to a neighbour everyday after school. I used to go there with a pint of milk in a can and had to tip it into a jug outside the lady's door, then take the can back to the farm and wash it ready for the next day. I got ninepence (4p) a week for that which was quite a lot of money. I had to give my mother sixpence (2½p), and kept thrupence for myself.

Phyllis Gibbins (born 1915)

We Drove the Wagon From Rowhedge to Colchester
I left school when I was fourteen and went to work for Mr Fale, the carrier, at Rowhedge. The wagon was made of wood and had the name 'T.W. Fale' (late Harris) on the side. It had a rack on the roof and we would take a lot of things on top. We charged about tuppence (1p) to take a parcel to town, and would do a lot of shopping for people - especially during the war when we would have to queue at the shops, which took time, and we would be late home. Sometimes we would collect orders from people's homes, or some would bring their parcels to us, or maybe wait for us on the road as we went past. When we got to Old Heath we'd often stop to pick up laundry that some local women had been doing for people in town. When we got to town we would stable the horse at the Plough Inn in Magdalen Street while we attended to our business.

Jack Austin (born 1907)

It Was Just Like a Shed on Wheels
Mr Fale ran a carrier service from Rowhedge. The vehicle was like a shed on wheels, motorised, with seats all the way round and they would take people into town. There was no official bus stops, but if you stood at your gate they would stop for you.

Phyllis Gibbins (born 1915)

Keith Moss, December 2015.

Jack Austin, pictured in 1993.

Deliveries Were Made By Horse and Cart
We lived at 15 Speedwell Road and I can remember Bert the baker coming round to deliver bread in a horse and cart, and he often used to stop outside our house, put a hay bag on the horse's head, and come inside for a cup of tea. One day when Bert went back out he found that the horse had gone and it finished up on the green by the Bell, just opposite Mason's shop. The horse was eating the grass in front of the house. The coalman also used to deliver coal with his horse and cart, and then on some Saturday mornings we used to nip down to the gasworks at the Hythe and get a big sack of coke for about a shilling (5p) and bring it back home on an old pram, or something. We would break it up with a hammer and put it on the fire which was a lot cheaper than just burning coal.

Keith Moss (born 1934)

I Had a Ride on the Coal Cart
We had the coalman, the oilman, the baker, the milkman and they all came in a horse and cart from the Co-op in Wimpole Road. The coalman would unload the coal in a big bunker outside the French windows. I can remember coming out of school one day and the coalman was coming along the road. He had a black face and he said to me, 'Hello Margaret, are you going home home now?' And I said that I was and he said, 'Would you like a ride?' Well I thought that was wonderful and he got down, picked me up and sat me up next to him on the coal cart and took me down the Old Heath Road and dropped me off outside our front gate.

Margaret Moss (1934)

We Had to Push the Bus Up the Hill
When I first started driving the motor bus we had no gearbox and would sometimes have trouble getting up Cannock Hill. And if we had too many passengers on board I would tell them to get off and we would have to push it up the hill. In that respect it wasn't quite so good as the horse that we previously had. When we did eventually get a gearbox we could go a bit quicker - maybe about 15-20 miles an hour. The bus had twelve seats and we charged thrupence (1p) to go from Rowhedge to Colchester. We stopped at every lamp post to pick up and drop off passengers and we did eight trips to town a day, finishing at ten o'clock at night.

Jack Austin (born 1907)

The Bus Used to Drop Us Off at Our Garden Gate
I can remember Fale's old brown Bedford bus coming past from Rowhedge on its way to Colchester. As kids we used to go into town on the bus and when we were coming home we just used to say to the driver, 'Mrs Allen's backyard please', and he would stop right outside our backyard. There were, of course, proper bus stops but the driver (Jack Austin from Rowhedge), would stop anywhere if he saw people standing for the bus, and the same would be true if you asked to be dropped off at a certain place.

Tony Gibbins (born 1940)

Tony Gibbins, January 2016.

A near deserted Old Heath Road apart from Fale's bus just passing the school en route to Colchester, c.1935

We Used to Help the Milkman With His Deliveries

We had a milkman called Mr Lord who lived at Place Farm and he used to deliver the milk with a horse and cart and my brother John and I would sometimes see him coming down the road and go and help him. Because people used to leave their jugs on the step John and I used to go and get the jug and then take it to Mr Lord, who would have a metal measure with a hook on it, and he would put it into the churn and and measure out a pint of milk before putting it into the customer's jug. We would then go and put it back on the customer's step. And I can remember going back with him to Place Farm on the horse and cart and he coming out with a tin of home-made toffee and giving us a big piece each.

Janet Rayner (born 1937)

I Worked at the Laundry for Five Shillings a Week

When I started at Old Heath Laundry I was getting five shillings (25p) a week, and my first job was in the ironing room. There was a machine in there where they would put the shirt on and I had to iron the collar, front, cuffs and sleeves, and then fold them up. I suppose there were about twenty of us there - mostly girls and some men. The irons that we used had gas jets inside them and they were lit before we got there so that they were nice and hot ready to start ironing.

Phyllis Gibbins (born 1915)

Interior view of Old Heath Laundry showing some of the pressing machines, c.1950s.

I Always Wanted to Be a Farmer
I always wanted to be a farmer from a very young age, and when I left school I got a job at Lexden Lodge for about a year before going to a farming college in Suffolk. After leaving college I rented eleven acres of land down Whitehall Road, from Percy Berryman, and it included all the farm buildings. In time, I rented further land and finished up with about 100 acres. I became a pig farmer and used to breed them and sell them on. I had to take them to Dunmow to be slaughtered. On the marshes I had cattle and sheep.

Keith Pettit (born 1934)

Keith Pettit, December 2015.

We Raised Hundreds of Chickens and Turkeys
When we first moved into Savill Cottage we had gas lighting to start and electricity came later. We kept all our incubators for hatching chickens and turkeys in the old schoolroom after which they were moved outside, and we kept hundreds of them. We had thirteen acres of land and my husband and I used to work this between us. We used to grow vegetables and deal in eggs and poultry. At Christmas time we used to supply Archer's, Mac Fisheries and Baughan's. Sometimes we would remove the furniture from one of the rooms in the house, cover it with newspaper, and then lay the chickens out in there. We would have hundreds of chickens on our land at any one time. In fact, I would often find that I couldn't hatch enough at a time so would have to buy some chicks in, mostly from Pleshey, and they would be sent by rail and have to be collected from the station.

Edith Johnson (born 1908)

I Used to Sell My Own Newspapers
In the latter years of my time at secondary school I had my own paper round. I used to go up to the printing place down the side of the Town Hall, where they used to print the late news on the back page, and I would buy 32 papers from them. I would then go up to the Regal cinema in Crouch Street where I would swap one of them for the Evening Star with the old boy who used to sell them there, and then cycle my way up to Lexden and deliver the papers. I had my own little round and I used to get three pound something a week out of that, which was more than what a paper boy could earn.

Steve Bailey (born 1948)

We Used to Have to Turn the Eggs Twice a Day
At Christmas time it was very hectic here because my mum had about a dozen large incubators in the old schoolroom where she used to hatch chicks - and there used to be over a thousand chicks come off quite regularly. And when we were children Wendy and I used to have to turn those eggs twice a day. Before the eggs were put into the incubators they were marked with a cross on one side, and a nought on the other, so that we knew which ones we had turned. The incubators would then be filled up with these eggs and it took three weeks for them to hatch.

Janet Read (born 1943)

I Was Paid About Four Pounds a Week
When I left school I managed to get a job at Gunton's in Crouch Street. I was interviewed for the job by Mr Geoffrey Gunton and I started practically the next week as soon as I had left school. I think that I got paid about four pounds a week - received in cash weekly. We used to get the orders up for what we called the 'posh people' - ladies who lived in Lexden Road. We would also serve in the shop although we never used to take money in them days - they used to have a lady who sat in a kiosk and the customers had to pay the money over to her. The kiosk was in the middle of the shop. I can also remember Mr Gunton's son Keith showing me how to bone a side of bacon - and I think that I could still do that today. It was while I was working at Gunton's that I met my future husband Pete who had been doing some building work there. One day he bought me a box of chocolates and that was that - and we ended up getting married in 1968. After I left Gunton's I got a job at Christian's in Old Heath. This was a general store which was opposite the fish and chip shop on Fingringhoe Road. I worked as a shop assistant and had to serve in the shop, fill up the shelves and do errands for Mr and Mrs Christian.

Sandra Bennett (born 1949)

Sandra Bennett, January 2016.

Cyril Johnson, pictured on his smallholding in Old Heath Road with his dog Curly, c.1960.

We Had Our Groceries Delivered Right Inside the House
I grew up in Wick Road and my name then was Mary Fisher. And I can remember that the Co-op baker, the butcher and the grocery man all used to do rounds. In fact, the grocery man used to take the key off the back of the loo door, let himself into the kitchen, leave the groceries where he'd been left a new order and some money, take the money, lock up again and off he'd go.

Mary Norman (born 1936)

Mary Norman, January 2016.

I Was Paid Seven Shillings a Week
I had a paper round at Claydon's, on the Old Heath Road opposite Cavendish Avenue, and used to deliver papers along Old Heath Road, D'arcy Road and up Abbot's Road - which was just a little lane in those days. I got paid seven shillings (35p) a week - that was a shilling a day, Monday - Saturday - plus an extra shilling on a Saturday because you had to collect your money. I used to get up at half past five in the morning and by half past seven I would be back home and over the Wick looking for rabbits.

Dick Jackson (born 1937)

Dick Jackson, January 2016.

I Can Remember My Paper Round Vividly

I started doing a paper round at Claydon's, where the Post Office is now, when I was about thirteen. And on my first day there I remember Bob Claydon taking me round in his new sports car because his mum and dad had just given him this wonderful car for his twenty-first birthday. I can remember my round vividly and could probably still recite most of the houses that I delivered to, and the papers that they had. I started off where Cottage Drive is now and would then go to the beginning of Fingringhoe Road and would go right down to the borough boundary and back again - including Foresight Road. And that was it, but it included about seventy or eighty houses. I remember that if we weren't there by half past six you got fined, which was probably against all the rules and regulations. I think that I got paid about eleven or twelve shillings (60p) a week, and if you did a Sunday, which I often did, you would get an extra couple of shillings

Martin Broom (born 1945)

Right: Martin Broom, aged eleven.

Below: Old Heath Road showing where the old Post Office was located set back among the row of houses on the right, c.1930. Note also the lack of any footpath on the left side of the road.

Fingringhoe Road looking towards Old Heath Road in the 1930s. Many will remember the old Fish and Chip shop seen here on the right side of the road.

Old Heath Road looking towards D'arcy Road in the 1930s. When this picture was taken the building on the immediate left side of the picture was an off licence run by Mr & Mrs Phillips. Note also the single car parked on the left hand side of the road - a far cry from the situation today

Chapter Six

Leisure & Events

Penny-farthing Bicycles Were in Common Use

When I was a young child penny-farthing bicycles were in common use, and I can well remember my cousin racing against another lad from the village on these solid unsprung machines. In those days our pleasures were few and our toys consisted of whips and tops, and also marbles. One of our greatest treats, however, was to go to the magic lantern show which was held every so often in the small chapel opposite the house where I lived. The anticipation of the magic lantern show was always intense and we talked about it for some time afterwards.

Alfred Mason (born 1878)

We Decided to Start a Social Club

Some years after I left school the people of Old Heath decided that they wanted to start a social club and they bought a piece of ground on the corner of D'arcy Road on which to build a clubhouse. They were charging one pound a foot for the land and we bought sixty foot. We then purchased an old army hut from Reed Hall for £60 and we went round collecting money to help pay for it. When we got it going we bought 120 chairs at five shillings each (25p), and we had a 'Tortoise' stove, just inside, for heating and we used to run whist drives with a dance afterwards. We charged sixpence (2½p) entrance and I used to sit at the door collecting all the money. In the end we decided to sell some shares in the club in order to raise some money to help pay off what we owed. We sold the shares for a pound each and General Skinner from Heathfields bought up several, and Doctor Reed at Old Heath Cottage did the same, so in the end we were able to pay everybody off with no money owing. Some time later, however, General Skinner was moving away and he gave all his shares to the church, and Doctor Reed did the same, and what few shares that we had left became worthless because they outnumbered us. So that hut ended up belonging to St Barnabas' Church and that was how we lost it.

Fred Johnson (born 1902)

We Had No Television, Radio or Record Players

When I was young there was no television, no radio or record players. My aunt Lizzie had a cylinder gramophone. The cylinders were in big cases which you had to take out and put on the gramophone. We used to have family sing-songs and would sing all sorts of songs and hymns. I also used to read a lot - I was always a big reader. I also used to cycle a lot, all round and into town. And sometimes I used to get my wheel caught in the tramlines.

Flossie Lappage (born 1905)

The Old Heath Social Club Was Erected by Local Volunteers
From the time I left school until just after the First World War, the land on which I am now living [215 Old Heath Road] was just an open field and sometime around 1920 it was sold off into building plots. One of these plots was on the corner of where D'arcy Road is now and Major General Skinner, who lived at Heathfields (formerly known as The Limes), was interested in starting a social club. So he purchased this plot of land and somehow we got the money together, with lots of people supporting it, and bought an old army hut and had an extension put on the front. It was erected on concrete piles because the land was low and the water collected there. It was actually put up by local volunteers including one or two decent carpenters. I can remember one instance when they were putting the roof on and too many people were concentrating on one particular place and the whole lot caved in. Eventually, however, we got started with the social club and had a billiard table, bagatelle table and a stage. We used to organise dances, whist drives and concert parties, and we eventually joined the Colchester Social Clubs League where you had a team playing whist, cribbage and darts.

Les Crick (born 1906)

You Always Wore Your Best Clothes on a Sunday
On a Sunday night in Colchester we would walk up and down the High Street after the girls. You put your best clothes on - you never walked out on a Sunday with your working clothes on. Everywhere you went you had to walk in those days and in the evenings we would often congregate outside Mason's shop. We would also sometimes go to the social club on the corner of D'arcy Road. They had a little bar there where you could buy lemonade, bars of chocolate and biscuits. They also had a dart board, table tennis and a half size billiard table.

Bob Allen (born 1906)

Members of the Old Heath Sports and Social Club outside their clubhouse, c.1922. Pictured from the left are: Les Crick, Reg Pettican, Eddie Allen (rear), Bob Allen (front), Eddie Amos and Mr Brindle.

PARTICULARS

OLD HEATH, COLCHESTER.

With the consent of the Charity Commissioners.

THE

FREEHOLD PROPERTY

KNOWN AS

The Old Heath Parish Room

Situate on the West side of Old Heath Road, at the corner of D'Arcy Road, the site having a frontage to Old Heath Road of 60 feet and a return frontage to D'Arcy Road of about 190 feet.

THE ACCOMMODATION COMPRISES :

Assembly Room (59ft. 6in. by 20ft.) with platform and slow combustion stove ;

Committee Room (18ft. by 9ft. 9in.) with slow combustion stove and coal bunker ;

Kitchen with sink, gas point and shelving :

Ladies' Cloakroom and W.C. adjoining ;

Men's Cloakroom with lavatory basin and W.C. adjoining.

Gas, Electricity, Council Water Supply and Main Drainage.

50
60
70
80
85
90
95
100
105
110
115
120 a...
125
130
135
140

Fredr George
Walker

89 East Hill
£140.

Above: Entry from a sale catalogue recording the sale of the Old Heath Parish Room for £140.

Below: Old Heath Road showing the Old Heath Parish Room on what is now the corner of D'arcy Road.

They Thought That the World Was Coming to an End

In 1884 an earthquake shook the district of Old Heath causing great alarm. People rushed out into the street and crowded together like a flock of frightened sheep. Many thought that the world was coming to an end. Although no buildings collapsed, a large number of roof slates were shaken down. However, mercifully, we all came through alive and uninjured. That Tuesday was a bright and sunny morning and I had been sent by my mother down the hill to my father's market garden to collect some vegetables. It was a cauliflower she wanted and we were going to have it for lunch. I reached my father's place just after nine o'clock and after I had collected the cauliflower from my father I set back up the hill again. There weren't many people about and I was just in front of the Bell [public house] when I heard this tremendous rattling noise. The ground also began to shake beneath my feet and I thought that I was going to be knocked over and the cauliflower fell out of my hand. The noise was all around me and I had no idea what it was. I just couldn't move and as I stood there the slates began to rattle off the roofs of the houses on both sides of the road. Some of the chimney stacks were falling as well, and there were big cracks in the walls. It didn't last long, but the rattling sound is something I'll never forget.

Alfred Mason (born 1878)

The Bell Inn undergoing repair work following damage caused by the earthquake of 1884.

We Used to Play With Live Bullets
The soldiers used to fire all their bullets from trenches in the ground over the Wick and when they had stopped firing we used to nip over there to see if we could find some of those live bullets. We would then take these bullets and make a hole in the bark of a tree and push them in. We then used to get our catapults, with some stones, and see if we could hit these bullets. And if you hit one it didn't half go up. I remember on one occasion my eldest brother blew the top of his thumb off playing around with these bullets in the shed. He had one of them in a vice and was trying to tap the top off the bullet.

Steve Mason (born 1906)

We Went Camping at Fingringhoe Wick
Miss Beryl Aldous decided to start a Girl Guides group from Donyland Lodge and they were going round to everyone who had girls asking if they wanted to join. I would have been about eleven or twelve by then and wanted to join. But my father had died and it was a question of being able to afford to buy the uniform. In the end my mother offered to make all the uniforms and, as a result, I got my uniform for free. We used to meet for Girl Guides in a farm building at Donyland Lodge. I was in the 'Forget Me Nots' and we finished up with about four patrols and were known as the First Old Heath Company. At meetings we would have a parade and were all inspected. There were four of five in a patrol, depending on the number attending. We learned to tie knots, Morse code, first aid and dancing. We also went camping down at Fingringhoe Wick. It cost about ten shillings (50p) a week to go to camp which included all the food, hire of the ground and probably the hire of the tents - I don't know how my mother paid for it but I really enjoyed myself. It was the first holiday that I'd had.

Phyllis Gibbins (born 1915)

We Used to Go Skipping Over the Park at Easter Time
We all used to have skipping ropes and as we got older, at Easter time, we would go down to the Castle Park. The park would be absolutely full of groups skipping - young ones, teenagers and older ones. That was a regular thing and I don't know when it stopped. You had to have a heavy rope and you would skip in a group - one would go in the rope, then go round, and then go in again. Skipping in the park was a regular thing at Easter.

Edna Mills (born 1918)

Phyllis Gibbins, aged eighteen in her Girl Guides uniform.

My Father Would Bet On Anything

My father's name was John Brewer Johnson and when he was younger he lived with his parents at the Lord Raglan public house on Military Road. When he moved to Old Heath he would often go to the Bell Inn and on one occasion he had a wager with someone there that he could kill, pluck, draw and cook a chicken so that it was fit to eat in half an hour. The wager was for ten shillings (50p), which was a lot of money at that time, and now he had to prove it. So he got the landlady of the Bell to get ready a big tin of boiling fat so that it was nice and hot. He then took one of his chickens up to the Bell, killed it by breaking its neck, plucked it (he could pluck a chicken in two minutes), drew it and then put it into the boiling fat. When he thought that it was ready he took it out and put it onto the counter before cutting it up to show that it was cooked right through - all within the time allowed. So he won his ten bob (shillings). My father would bet on anything.

Fred Johnson (born 1902)

We Used to Practically Live Over the Wick

We used to practically live over the Wick. There used to be a gang of us that used to play together and mum didn't mind us going out as long as we were with a group - we were not allowed to go on our own. There would be a whole crowd of us - boys as well as girls. I remember on one occasion one of the boys had a box of matches with him and he set fire to the gorse bushes and we all ran away, and the flames were really high and someone sent for the police. And, of course, the boy responsible told the police that he hadn't done it, but when the policeman had gone he told his mum that it was him, but he wouldn't say it to the policeman.

Gladys Rudd (born 1927)

We Used to Go and Watch the Military Bands

On Sunday mornings we would sometimes go to watch the military bands coming out of Camp Church and marching on the parade ground. There was a big square there and as they came out of church they would gather on the parade ground. Each regiment had a band and they would march off to join their band. It was a lovely sight, and nice to see all the fashions that people were wearing. It used to be packed on the roadway inside the camp - probably hundreds of people. Soldiers in their colourful uniforms - sometimes quick marching, sometimes slow marching. That was a regular parade.

Edna Mills (born 1918)

Soldiers in full dress uniform marching in to Camp Church, c.1914

74

Above: The Bell Inn (c.1930) where John Brewer Johnson took on an interesting wager (see opposite page). The roof to the right side of the picture was renewed following the earthquake of 1884.

Below: John Brewer Johnson seen here in his pony and trap outside the Lord Raglan public house in Military Road, c.1900

We Had a Lot of Military Ground in Old Heath

We would go out on our own because we had all this military ground in Old Heath. We used to play over the Wick and firing ranges and take picnics, light fires and cook things. There was a little stream that we went through and we would sometimes dam it up and try to swim in it. The boys used to go down to the Roman river with these fuel tanks that had been dropped from aircraft. They would cut them up a bit, line them with sandbags, paint them up and use them as canoes.

Joy Cardy (born 1934)

We Used to Listen to Dick Barton on the Radio

We never had a television in those days but we did have a radio. And we used to listen to programmes such as *Dick Barton: Special Agent* and Simon Templar in *The Saint*, and various other comedy shows that were on. We would also play a lot of games such as Ludo and Snakes and Ladders, and also cards. We also had a dart board for playing darts and we also used to play a game called High Cockalorum. Someone would bend over against a wall and the others would take a run from the kitchen and jump up on their back, and so on and you would see how many could get on there without falling off. Every time someone jumped onto someone's back he would shout out 'High Cockalorum - Chic Chic Chic.

Keith Moss (born 1934)

The River Was Chock-a-block With Barges

It used to be a regular thing on a Sunday evening to go down to the river to see all the Thames barges which would be anchored along the quay for the weekend. And the river was almost chock-a-block full with barges down both sides. Sometimes we would walk along the river as far as Rowhedge. I can also remember the shunting engine from Hythe railway station coming along the road and taking coal directly to the gas works and the electricity station. You used to be able to go down to the gas works and buy creosote.

Frank Gooding (born 1931)

We Always Played Games at Parties

My father was wonderful at parties and always had a game for us to play. One game that we used to play was called 'The Family Coach'. My dad would tell a story about a horse and carriage that was going somewhere and everyone would be assigned a character from the story. So for example, if you were the horse and he mentioned the word 'Horse' in the story, you would have to stand up, turn around, and sit down again. Or if you were the coachman and he mentioned him in the story you would have to stand up, turn around, and sit down again. And If you didn't do it you would have to pay a forfeit. And, of course, he used to say this all very quickly and you would be standing up, turning round and sitting down again all in a hurry.

Margaret Moss (born 1934)

I Joined the Girl Guides When I Was Eleven

I joined the Girl Guides when I was eleven years old and we used to hold our meetings in Donyland Lodge. We had to go through the cattle shed where the cows were kept, and then go up some steps to the room at the top. It was the First Old Heath Group and about twenty girls attended. We learned how to make things for camp such as making stands for wash basins and how to hang clothes up in the middle of the tent - all with pieces of wood and string. When it came to paying for our uniforms we had a card and would perhaps pay sixpence (2½p) a week. I'm still associated with the Guides today as a member of the Handicapped Trefoil Guild, and we help to raise funds for the Colchester Trefoil.

Edna Mills (born 1918)

Thames sailing barges line the quay side at the Hythe in this view from the early 1900s.

We Used To Play Cricket in the Road

We used to spend most of our spare time outside, especially in the summer. Most evenings would probably be spent playing cricket down the middle of Rowhedge Road. At other times we might go and sit on the style at the end of the lane [by Place Farm] and just chat. And, of course, there weren't many cars around at that time. When I got to about thirteen or fourteen I took up cycling with a few of my friends from around Speedwell Road way, and we used to go off cycling all over the place. In the evenings we would probably go down to West Mersea - that was a favourite trip. And then at weekends we could be going anywhere because I used to belong to the Colchester Cycling Club. Probably on a Sunday morning we would have a time trial travelling up to perhaps Bury-St-Edmunds. We would cycle up there, stay in bed and breakfast overnight, and then race in the morning before cycling home. I carried on doing that for about ten or twelve years.

Tony Gibbins (born 1940)

I Used to Attend the Co-op Youth Club

In the evening we would often sit down and listen to Dick Barton on the radio. We had the radio on a lot and would sit there in the evenings listening to plays while my mother did the ironing. We had just one light fitting and there would a lead going down to the radio, and another to the iron, and the light fitting would be swinging backwards and forwards because there were no electric sockets in the wall - all you had was the light fitting and you plugged everything into that. I was also a member of the Pathfinders group that used to meet in the old wooden hut on the corner of D'arcy Road. It was a club for younger children where they could meet and play games. When you got to fourteen you could join the Co-op youth club. We had at table tennis table and a billiard table, and we also used to go on outings to places like Mersea on our bikes. I remember that someone had given the club a radiogram which we had on the stage,and we managed to buy a record to play on it which was *A Slow Boat to China*, and we danced to that one record every evening. Half way through the evening we would go into the kitchen and would make some toast with melted cheese which cost us a ha'penny a slice. The club was run by Mr Mason.

Margaret Moss (born 1934)

We Used to Go to the Saturday Morning Pictures

It used to cost sixpence to get into the Saturday morning pictures. I tried to become a monitor because then you could get in free, but I never managed to become one. The Hippodrome was the first place that we used to go to. The films included Smiling Jack, Batman and then all the cowboy pictures. When we came out it used to be a penny bus ride home to Old Heath. We always used to have tuppence (1p) to buy some chips with, so we used to buy tuppence worth of chips from the fish and chip shop in Vineyard Street, and then we'd walk over to Stanwell Street to a little shop called Robinson's - which was a bakers, where you could buy two crusty rolls for a penny. We would then hook the dough out and stuff our chips into the rolls. We used to do that every Saturday. And then, of course, having spent our penny bus fare on the rolls, we would have to walk home.

Dick Jackson (born 1937)

The Kids Used to Make a Lot of Noise

Sometimes we would go to the Saturday morning pictures where there would be crowds of kids making a lot of noise. We used to go to the Playhouse and we would all sing along to the words which were written up on the screen. There would be a main film and also a serial of some sort which always ended in a cliffhanger so you had to return the following week to find out what had happened. As I got older I would go out dancing on a Saturday night - either to the Corn Exchange or perhaps the Albert. There would be a band playing and this is where young girls could meet young boys. On Sunday night we would always go to the Jazz Club at the Civil Service Club, and on Monday night it was always the Rock 'n Roll Club at Paxman's - so it was three nights on the trot.

Janet Rayner (born 1937)

The Hippodrome cinema was a popular venue for Saturday morning pictures.

We Used to Cheer the Goodies and Boo the Baddies

On Saturday mornings we used to get the No 6 bus from the end of the road which would take us into town and we would go to the Saturday morning pictures at the Hippodrome, which I think cost us sixpence (2½p) to get in. We used to thoroughly enjoy ourselves. They used to have two serials - something like Gene Autry - and the audience would cheer the goodies and boo the baddies, and they would have a feature film which was often a cowboy. I can also remember going to watch a Lone Ranger film at the old Empire on Mersea Road with my parents after school one day.

Stephen Cudmore (born 1947)

We Went To the Rainbow Club

I used to belong to the Co-op junior club which was called 'The Rainbows' and we met in the old wooden hut on the corner of D'arcy Road. It was run by Dorothy Jennings and we used to go there and make things and play games. This was when I was still at school and I remember that we had a badge to wear which was all the different colours of the rainbow.

Janet Read (born 1943)

I Used to Keep and Breed Rabbits

I joined the Old Heath Rabbit Club which was run by a Mr Partridge who lived in Whitehall Road, and also Mr Hindle who was headmaster of the school. There were about 25 people in the group and we used to meet at Mr Partridge's house in Whitehall Road. We all used to keep and breed rabbits and show them.

Keith Pettit (born 1934)

The Playhouse in St John's Street was also a popular venue for Saturday morning pictures.

We Would Spend All Day Playing on the Wick

In the summer time we were never at home - we were always over the Wick. We used to go down Wick Lane and across the Wick to the Butts where the soldiers used to do the firing, and then on the back field, which was open, we used to play football. We would take bottles of water, or cold tea, and a sandwich and we would generally be away all day - we would never go home at lunch time. Sometimes we would take a few potatoes along with us and put them in some water, light a fire, and cook these potatoes for our dinner. On Sunday mornings about ten of us would go over the Wick to play football. We would pick a side and would sometimes finish up with thirty or forty playing as more and more turned up. We also used to play football at other places on a Saturday morning which would often include members of the well-known local Hunt family. There would be Derek, Peter, Ronnie, Billy and Bobby. Derek went on to play football for Ipswich Town, Ronnie played for Colchester United, Billy, I think, played for Colchester United Reserves and, of course, Bobby - who was a lot younger - also played for the U's.

Keith Moss (born 1934)

We Played a Lot of Football in Our Spare Time

We used to play a lot of football in our spare time. Those at the top end of Speedwell Road and those at the bottom end had their own football teams, and we would sometimes play matches. On a Sunday at what I call the bottom end of the road, where we lived at 87 Speedwell Road, was a field at the back and it was nothing unusual to have about twelve or perhaps fifteen on each side. And whoever had the football had the first pick. The Hunts would be there because they all played football, except for Bobby at that time because he was a lot younger. Billy Hunt and I were mates because we used to go to training at Colchester. Ronnie Hunt, who went on to play for the U's, was built like a brick wall and if you tackled him you knew all about it.

Dick Jackson (born 1937)

Young footballers from the Speedwell Road area line up for this group photograph in the late 1940s.
Back row: Peter Keeble, Keith Moss, Peter Hunt, Nelson Blowers, Ronald Farrow, Alec Nevard.
Front row: Dougie Oliver, Gordon Buck, Gerry Wanford, Tommy Moorcroft, Hugh Harvey.

Paste Sandwiches and Home Made Lemonade

From around the age of eight we could be out over the Wick all day. We would just take some jam or paste sandwiches and a bottle of home made lemonade - just some sherbert put it into a bottle of water - and we would be gone for the whole day. Very few people had cars in those days so we used to spend a lot of our time playing in the road. We would play hopscotch or rounders and if ever we heard a bus or anything come along we would just stop and wait until it had gone. One particular game that we used to play was called 'Tracking'.We would leave one or two at the starting point and then the rest of us would go off and leave arrows, with a piece of chalk, showing the way that we were going, and we had to try and get back to where we had started from before they found us. And often we would put the arrow pointing in the opposite direction to where we were going, or perhaps in both directions. here may have been about ten of us playing and we might have ventured as far as Rowhedge, or the sand pit. We just used to have fun then.

Sandra Bennett (born 1949)

Sandra Bennett, aged seven

I Remember Playing Football With Bobby Hunt

We used to play over the Wick a lot and we would meet other children there from all round the area. I remember playing football with Bobby Hunt. He was somewhat older than us and he would put about six of us in goal and shoot at us. He was pretty good. I remember on one occasion going to the Recreation Ground to watch Old Heath school play when I was about eight or nine. And Bobby Hunt was playing and I think that they won 13-0, and Bobby Hunt scored eleven or twelve of them - he was that good. But there were also some quite good players in my own year, including David and Alan Buck who were in my class. Alan played in goal for Colchester in later years and David played to quite a good standard as well.

Martin Broom (born 1945)

We Made Dens and Played On Distillery Pond

We often used to play in the woods at the laundry which is now all built on. We used to make dens and we would often find lots of 'left overs' from the war, such as drinking containers and helmets. We would occasionally find old fuel tanks which had been jettisoned from the aircraft, and we would try to put these fuel tanks onto the pond and make boats out of them. On other occasions we would get some five gallon drums, lash them together, and make rafts and go out onto Distillery Pond and fish from them.

Steve Bailey (born 1948)

Bullets Were Whizzing Around

I can remember walking right over to the Butts and hearing bullets whizzing around - which didn't worry us at the time and how close they were I wouldn't know. They used to have red flags flying warning of the danger but we never took any notice of them. We would go into the Butts themselves and dig around in the sand trying to find some spent bullets. We also used to go and look at the positions where they fired them from and look for the spent shell casings. We used to collect those and whistle through them.

Martin Broom (born 1945)

We Played Cricket and Rounders in the Road

We used to spend a lot of our time over the Wick because where we lived we were handy for that. We used to play cowboys and indians and as we got older we used to take our bikes across and play at scrambling. You could also play out in the road in those days. We often used to play cricket or rounders in Cavendish Avenue, or even football. You could set your pitch up in the road because there were so few vehicles about, it was quite safe. Our parents didn't mind us going out on our own. People didn't worry about you being abducted or knocked over on the road in those days.

Stephen Cudmore (born 1947)

Left: Martin Broom, 1951

Right: Stephen Cudmore, 1952

Below: The firing ranges in February 2016

The Girls Were Divided into Fairy Rings

I first got involved with the Old Heath Brownie Group through my sister Joan. The existing Pack Leader was going to retire and Joan was going to take over as Brown Owl. My mother was Tawny Owl and I was a Pack Leader. So it was very much a family affair. We used to meet in Old Heath School on Friday evenings at six o'clock. We met in the main hall and had about twenty four Brownies in the group made up from girls aged between six and ten years old. We would start off with all the Brownies divided into the fairy ring. The Brownies would all be divided into their little groups - fairies, pixies, elves, imps and gnomes and they would go into their corner of the room, and then you would call them into the fairy ring. You would then check that each one was there and that you had collected the subs. And then we had games, part of their promise and their law, and then we would do all sorts of different things - flags, stitching, knots, and all various things that they had to learn in their little groups. If someone was more advanced you would put them doing something different. We used to play games such as Lucy Locket where all the girls would sit in a circle on the floor singing the words to the rhyme, while one of them would walk round the outside before proclaiming that one of the girls had stolen Lucy's locket and put in in their pocket. All the Brownies had to learn a promise. This was to do their best, to do their duty to God and the Queen, and to help other people at all times. After this they were enrolled as a Brownie and got their badge.

Yvonne Barker (born 1941)

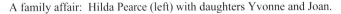

A family affair: Hilda Pearce (left) with daughters Yvonne and Joan.

Yvonne Barker (nee Pearce), December 2015.

We Sent Morse Code Signals From House to House

I belonged to the Cubs and also to the Scouts for a short while. I joined the Cubs when I was about eight years old and we used to meet at Old Heath School. We were known as the Twenty-first Colchester and had Brian Mead as the young Cub leader, and Brian Slowgrove as the Scout Master. The cub pack was quite a large group and we were divided into packs called Sixers. We all had to wear a uniform and at meetings we would play a lot of quite robust games, which I quite enjoyed. We had to learn such subjects as knot-making and Morse code and I can remember sitting at home in my bedroom at 16 D'arcy Road and flash across the road to somebody else, who in turn, would flash to somebody else so we could send messages down the road. We weren't always very accurate but I can remember being able to do Morse code at one time.

Martin Broom (born 1945)

We Were Taught How to Wash Up and Do Basic Cooking

I started off in the Brownies and later went up to the Guides. The Brownies group was called the Second Old Heath Brownies and we attended one evening a week. We learnt how to tie knots, how to lay a table, the correct order to wash up and a bit of basic cookery. When I was in the Guides we used to go camping and I remember going to Danbury Park on one occasion and we were all under canvas. Our transport there was in a furniture van which had a tailgate where we would clamber aboard, and there would be about twenty of us rolling about in the back of the van.

Janet Rayner (born 1937)

Above: Janet Rayner, November 2015.

Left: Janet Rayner pictured in her Brownies uniform alongside her brother John who was a member of the Boys' Brigade.

We Were All Old Heath Girls and Knew Each Other

I started off in the Brownies at Old Heath. Our Brown Owl was Joan Pearce who lived in D'arcy Road and her mother was Tawny Owl. And then I flew up to the Guides at which time you were given your wings to wear to show that you had received your first class Brownies badge. We used to meet in Old Heath School about six o'clock in the evening. And then with the Guides we still met at the school with Miss Sizer who was the Guide Captain. We used to do tracking in the summer and two of the Guides used to go off over the Wick and would lay a trail with different sized stones - such as a big stone and a little stone placed in a certain way indicating the way they had to go. We also used to do marching and, of course, we used to go to Guide camp. We went to Kelvedon one year and Gosfield another year - we never went too far away. Only one year did we go to Kent. We would stay away for about a week at a time. I loved the Guides and stayed in it until I left school. It was a very thriving group and, of course, we were all Old Heath girls so we all knew each other.

Janet Read (born (1943)

Above: This group of Brownies is pictured in the school playground sometime in the late 1950s. On the right of the picture can be seen Yvonne Pearce (pack leader), standing next to her mother Hilda Pearce (Tawny Owl). Standing to the left of the picture is Brenda Blowers (pack leader)

Below: This group of young performers are seen at Co-op Hall sometime around 1950.
Back row: Kathleen Scales, Kay Syrett, Janice Clarke, Mary Boyd, Margaret Rogers, Janet Scales, Carol Crosby
Front row: (?), Janet Brazier, Wendy Read, (?) Brenda Blowers, Marion Cornwall, Janet Read

We Played Games Such as British Bulldog
I was a member of the Twenty-first Colchester Scouts Group at Old Heath and we used to meet at the school every Monday evening. We all wore yellow neckerchiefs and Robert Schofield from Wimpole Road was Skip and lots of local boys used to attend, including some from Rowhedge. We had to wear a uniform which included shorts in those days. We did a lot of badge work, as well as camping preparation and, of course, games such as British Bulldog. You started off with just one person in the middle of the hall and everybody else would line up at one end and they had to run from one end to the other, without getting caught by the person in the middle who would do his best to grab hold of you. If you got caught you had to then join the catcher in the middle and help him to catch the others. So you can imagine it got quite rough at times.

Stephen Cudmore (born 1947)

We Sold Our Blackberries to Mrs Johnson
We used to go blackberry picking over Friday Woods and then we used to take them to Mrs Johnson [opposite the school] who would buy them from us and she would then sell them on to her customers, or to the local shops. She used to weigh them and give us pocket money for them which we would then spend on sweets in the local shops. As I got older I also used to go pea picking at Battleswick Farm and at the end of the day they would weigh what you had picked and you would get paid.

Sandra Bennett (born 1949)

Elocution Lessons
I used to attend elocution lessons at Old Heath with a Miss York. And occasionally she used to put on concerts featuring her pupils in the Methodist Church by the Recreation Ground. And I remember performing there and reciting *The King's Breakfast.* Miss York lived at the top of Barn Hall Avenue and I would go to her home for my lessons. The tuition was on a one to one basis.

Mary Norman (born 1936)

I Remember the Fire at the Co-op Hall
I can remember being woken up by my mum and dad and being told, 'Come and look at this', and being taken to our front bedroom window and looking up the road and seeing the flames of the Co-op Hall as it was burning. And then the next morning we walked up there and saw all the blackened timbers. That must have been about 1951 and I seem to remember it being quite badly damaged.

Martin Broom (born 1945)

The old Co-op hall the morning after the fire, 1 December 1950.

86

I Used to Go All Over the Place on My Scooter

When I was working at Severalls Hospital I bought a scooter from a place on North Hill. I had never ridden a scooter before and the man from the shop took me down to the bottom of Castle Park where he twice rode back and forth across that field, with me on the back, before I was allowed to ride it home on my own. So off I went and when I got home I managed to fall off and damage the scooter, although thankfully my father said that he would get it repaired for me. It was a Vespa scooter and I used to go all over the place on it - sometimes with my brother John on the back. I used to travel to Gloucestershire on it and up to Norfolk, and I can only remember coming off on two occasions. I ended up selling it to my brother John who went on his honeymoon on it.

Mary Norman (born 1936)

Mary Norman (nee Fisher) on her Vespa scooter in Wick Road with her friend Joan Platt on the back. Joan was to later marry Mary's brother John and become her sister-in-law. c.1960

Old Heath Ladies Group

I'm involved nowadays with the Old Heath Ladies Group and we meet on the first and third Thursday evening of each month. We have speakers at most meetings, or if not we will play bingo or any other game that we can find. Sometimes we might have a beetle drive or perhaps just a social evening. We also have a Christmas meal and a summer strawberry fayre. We meet in the church hall and have between twenty and thirty in attendance at most meetings .

Sandra Bennett (born 1949)

Fancy Dress Party

I was ten years old at the time of the Coronation Tea Party. It was held in Cavendish Avenue and it was a fancy dress party. Those in fancy dress paraded all around Cavendish Avenue and Canwick Grove and then in the evening, on a piece of land opposite to Canwick Grove, they had a staging built and a band was playing and there was dancing in the street. All the children were given a propelling pencil with the crown and ER written on it - and I still have my pencil.

Janet Read (born 1943)

Janet Read holding her souvenir Coronation pencil.

The judging is about to begin in the Coronation fancy dress parade at Old Heath in June 1953.

I Helped to Start the Old Heath Friendship Club

Myself and another lady started up what came to be the Old Heath Friendship Club, and later the Townswomen's Guild. We sent notices to anyone we thought might be interested and contacted the Co-op to see if we could use the hall one afternoon a week for a meeting. We decided to give it a go and charged 50p as a subscription. We tried it for six months to see if it was worth doing and then had to put the subscription up because we had as many as sixty members. So that is how the Friendship Club started. At first we didn't have speakers and used to play bingo or beetle.

Phyllis Gibbins (born 1915)

St Barnabas Young Wives Club

Sometime after I got married I helped to form the St Barnabas Young Wives Club, probably sometime in the 1960s. We were a group of ladies who didn't want to belong to the Women's Union, so we got together and we used to organise various speakers to come and give us a talk on various subjects. Plenty of people used to come along to the meetings and we would also go out on trips on occasions. I remember one time we all went to the Red Lion and had a meal. We used to meet in the old church hall and we would have around forty people present on some occasions.

Maureen Ruddock (born 1935)

Members of the Old Heath Young Wives Group enjoying a meal at the Red Lion Hotel, c.1970.

Left (from front): A. Chittock, J. Hammond, E. Naylor, A. Taylor, (?) E. Southernwood (rear), S. Beard, H. Sutton, A. Harvey

Right (from front): Mrs Callaghan, M. Ruddock, B. Beale, M. Tucker, Mrs Bean, P. Shepherd, .E. Mills, (?)

Back (from left): (?) (?) B. Harris, C. Claydon

Front (from left) (?) M. Watts, W. Turner

I Was Made a Freeburgess of Colchester

In October 2015 I was made a Freeburgess of the town which is an old custom dating back to King Richard I. This was because my father had the privilege of being one, as well as my grandfather and my great grandfather. Formerly the privilege was only passed down to the sons of the families, but three years ago they changed the rules so that daughters were allowed to become one as well, so I applied and was accepted. And my daughter Suzanne also applied and she was also made a Freeburgess. At the ceremony we had to swear on the Bible that we were speaking the truth.

Janet Read (born 1943)

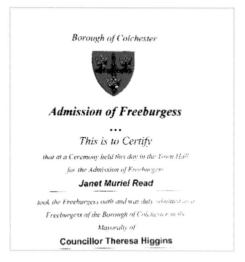

Borough of Colchester

Admission of Freeburgess
...
This is to Certify
that at a Ceremony held this day in the Town Hall
for the Admission of Freeburgess
Janet Muriel Read
took the Freeburgess oath and was duly admitted as a
Freeburgess of the Borough of Colchester in the
Mayoralty of
Councillor Theresa Higgins

Part of the certificate conferring Freeburgess rights to Janet Read, October 2015.

Here are some Old Heath youngsters having fun in D'arcy Road in the winter of 1949.
Pictured from the left are: Maureen Bridges, Colin Usher, Clive Jackson, Janet Bridges and Mariette Porter.

90

Garden Party at Buckingham Palace

I got an invitation to attend a garden party at Buckingham Palace in May 2012. It was in connection with my volunteer work with the Royal Association for Deaf People in Colchester. It was an absolutely lovely day and you could walk around the beautiful grounds. And then the Queen and Prince Philip came along chatting to the people. And I happened to be in a position right at the front and could see everybody including Prince William and Kate, Princess Anne and Prince Edward. It was a lovely experience and we had our tea. That was one of the highlights of my life and the very next day I got married to my husband.

Margaret Madden (born 1944)

Right: Margaret Madden (nee Mills), December 2015.

Below: This dance group used to meet in the Co-op Hall and were taught by a person called Jean Butcher, believed to be the lady in the centre wearing a striped top. The group includes young Margaret Mills who can be seen third from the right in the back row of those seated, wearing a small white head garland.

Chapter Seven

Further Reflections

The Oil Lamps Were Lit in the Street Every Night
Sometime around 1892, about the time I was leaving school, street lamps, using oil, were being installed in Old Heath. There were about ten of these lamps and my father was put in charge. He had to carry a ladder and had to ensure that the lamps were lit at a certain time, maintained and then extinguished at a later hour. The wages for this job were ten shillings (50p) a week.

Alfred Mason (born 1878)

There Was a Beautiful Avenue of Trees
We used to reckon that Old Heath was the area around the Bell public house, but the Old Heath postal area was thought to start near Cannock Mill on the Old Heath Road. From Cannock Mill up as far as Whitehall Road [now Whitehall Close] there was a beautiful avenue of trees - oaks and elms - big trees which met in the centre across the road. It was beautiful going through there in the summer and autumn times. There were no buildings along there at all until you got to Whitehall Road. On the opposite side of the road was a long drive leading to Whitehall which was owned by a Captain Ind. This was one of the larger houses in Old Heath and was set back from the road. At the entrance to the drive was Lodge Cottage, where the footman lived, whose name I believe was Hancox in those days. And I can remember the horse-drawn carriage coming out of the drive with the footmen standing on the carriage.

Les Crick (born 1906)

It Was All Horse Traffic
When I was a young lad it was all horse traffic. There were no buses or anything and there were very few motor bikes - everyone was on bicycles. And people used to clear all the horse manure up for their roses. Everybody had beautiful roses around this way. The horses were very well behaved and well trained. They would stand for hours - particularly if the driver liked a drink! The first thing he would do is tie the reins up and put a nosebag on the horse's head before going off into the pub. And when he came out a couple of hours later - probably the worse for wear - he would just take the nosebag off, grab hold of the reins and say 'Giddy-up' and the horse would take him home to wherever he had to go.

Steve Mason (born 1906)

People Today Are Never Satisfied
Looking back, people want so much today - they are never satisfied. We never had any trouble - you could leave your house open, you could walk about and you never had to worry about your purse. I suppose the fact that they have television and washing machines is better, but we never worried about such things. When we were first married we did have a wireless - it was one of those that you made yourself, or you got someone to make it for you. There were no washing machines in those days and you had to do everything by hand. You swept the floors and polished them because we didn't have a vacuum cleaner. But everybody was in the same boat.

Doris Thimblethorpe (born 1903)

The Way of Life is Now Much Easier
The way of life is now much easier. You don't have to light a fire before you can get a cup of tea in the morning. We have central heating here [Heathfields House] and a tumble dryer which makes things so much easier. The bad side of things are that the children haven't got the freedom and the pleasure that we had. They haven't got the 'Penny Rush' like they had at the Empire. Children sit down in front of the television all the time now, which isn't good. We used to go on the Wick and play games, but now parents are frightened to let their children out.

Edna Mills (born 1918)

We Had a Little Library in Old Heath
There was a carpenter and builder who had workshop in Fingringhoe Road, opposite the entrance to Wick Lane [now Wick Road]. His name was James Malster and he was also a coffin maker. Next to this were two houses - a white boarded house and a black boarded house. Mr Malster and his wife used to live in the white house and the black house was used as a laundry, and my mother used to work there as a laundress. And in front of where the laundry building stood was a little library which had been presented to the area by Sir Weetman Pearson - who later became Lord Cowdray. From my own memory it was just a small wooden building with ivy growing over it in my young days. And they used to have the daily newspapers available in there. Before the First World War Old Heath also had a village band and they used to practise in the old library - that was their band room for practising. The building used to be known as 'Pearson's Public Library'.

Les Crick (born 1906)

Old Heath Public Library which was opened in March 1892.

Old Heath Was Like a Village in My Childhood Days
Old Heath in my childhood days was a little community and was more like a village. The lamplighter used to come round with his pole and put the gas lights on. And then about eleven o'clock he came along and put them out. He lived in Speedwell Road and he used to tie his lamplighter's pole to his crossbar. And the street lights in Abbot's Road only went as far as the first gap in the Wick and then there were no more lights until you got to Mersea Road, and the trees used to meet in the middle of the road. When I was little I knew of just three cars in Old Heath. My parents had one, Mr Ardley, who had Place Farm, had one and a Mr Warne in Wick Road had a tiny little Austin.

Janet Read (born 1943)

We Didn't Have a Crossing Lady at the School
Old Heath has changed so much over the years. When I see all that traffic at the end of Abbots Road, I can't believe that it was just like a country road then. We didn't even have a crossing lady when I first started at the school. Only the headmaster had a car when I started and if I didn't cycle to school I used to go on the bus. And I have walked to school all the way from Shrub End when it was a very cold winter. And I would be absolutely glowing when I got there.

Anna Streatfield (born 1933)

There Were Very Few Cars on the Roads
When I first came to Old Heath School, Old Heath itself was very much a village where everyone knew everyone. And that's what I liked about it. Having been brought up in a village myself I really liked the atmosphere. There were much fewer cars on the roads and you never saw any cars parked outside the school and you never saw parents come to meet the children. We just used to let them go out and off they went home. As it got busier we did eventually have a crossing lady. I've got a feeling that perhaps one of the teachers used to see the little ones across the road, but I'm not absolutely sure about that.

Mary Bareham (born 1934)

A quiet looking Old Heath Road as seen in the early 1930s. To the left of the picture is where the entrance to Cottage Drive would later be built, and the house seen on the right is today's 354 Old Heath Road.

Cannock Mill Was a Flour Mill

Cannock Mill used to be owned by Mr Pulford who also ran the Bourne Mill site. They used to do quite a lot of grinding of corn and producing flour and other animal feed. It was a water mill supplied by a stream that came from Bourne Mill. From there the water went under the road and into Distillery Pond. They also used to keep pigs and cattle there. In fact, the cattle sheds are still there and have since been converted into a children's nursery. He used to graze his cattle on the field to the left of Old Heath Road leading up to Whitehall Road.

Les Crick (born 1906)

We Used to Pick it Up With a Shovel and Bucket

When the horse and carts used to come round with their deliveries they would sometimes leave their droppings behind, and if we happened to see them coming we used to get a shovel and a bucket and go outside and pick it up, because dad was always pleased to have it to put on the garden where he was growing his tomatoes. But you had to be quick because someone else might have spotted it and they would go out before you and beat you to it. It didn't stay on the road very long - that's for sure.

Janet Rayner (born 1937)

D'arcy Road Was Little More Than a Field

The gates that used to be across the bottom of D'arcy Road were never closed and were just hanging on their hinges. But it was really just a field in the early days which had originally been called Road Field, and then later, Walnutree Field. Finally, of course, it was renamed D'arcy Road. Most of my early memories of Old Heath was it being a place with not much traffic about. I can remember the little well by the road at the bottom of Cottage Drive. It was a small brick or concrete building by the side of the road that had water coming out of it and next to that was a little pond.

Maureen Ruddock (born 1935)

Old Heath Community Primary School 2002.   M Moss.

This excellent pen and ink drawing of Old Heath School, showing how it appeared in 2002, was drawn by local resident Margaret Moss.

An aerial view showing part of the Old Heath area in 2005.